Orlie Meskimen
Edited by Ellen Meskimen-Hustad

DEAR FOLKS, LOVE ORLIE
Orlie Meskimen Book, LLC

Copyright © 2017 by Ellen Meskimen-Hustad

All rights reserved. This book may not be reproduced in whole or in part, in any form (beyond copying permitted by Sections 107 and 108 of the United States Copyright Law, and except limited excerpts by reviewer for the public press), without written permission from Ellen Meskimen-Hustad.

Author services by Pedernales Publishing, LLC.
www.pedernalespublishing.com

Cover design: Jose Ramirez

Library of Congress Control Number: 2017909556

ISBN 978-0-9991347-0-2 Paperback Edition
ISBN 978-0-9991347-1-9 Hardcover Edition
ISBN 978-0-9991347-2-6 Digital Edition

Printed in the United States of America

TABLE OF CONTENTS

CHAPTER 1:
March 1941 – Camp Clairborne 1

CHAPTER 2:
January 1942 – Northern Ireland 81

CHAPTER 3:
January 1943 – North Africa 187

CHAPTER 4:
September 1943 – Italy 259

CHAPTER 5:
June 1944 – Return to the States 317

CHAPTER 6:
Epilogue 353

INTRODUCTION

Orlie Leroy Meskimen was born in a tiny cottage in Cedar Rapids, Iowa, on January 6, 1919, the only child of Clifford Leroy and Clara Rebecca (Mason) Meskimen.

When he was a young boy his parents moved to Shellsburg, Iowa, where although they were not wealthy, he enjoyed a happy childhood. His maternal grandmother, May Mason, also lived in the home with them. He loved her dearly. As a young boy during the Great Depression, he spent much of his time hunting and fishing, and for the most part enjoyed a Huck Finn childhood.

In high school he was a star basketball athlete. Following graduation he attended the University of Iowa for a brief time, studying chemical engineering, followed by employment with the Rock Island Railroad.

Orlie enlisted in the Iowa Army National Guard in December of 1940, and these letters begin shortly after his arrival at Camp Claiborne in early March of 1941.

Orlie Meskimen

This is his story taken from his letters. These letters were lovingly kept by his parents for over forty years before being discovered by his children while clearing out their grandparent's home.

Orlie stated in one of his letters that he wished to write a book when he returned from the war. He eventually made it home from the war, got married, and had five children. Life got busy and the book did not get written ... until now. Because of his letters, his book will now exist.

NOTE TO READERS: Orlie courted two women named LaVonne during the course of the war. In order to avoid confusion, one of the LaVonne's names has been changed to "Diane" In his letters.

While many of Orlie's letters were hand written, some were typed when a typewriter was available for his use. The letters in the Minion Pro font indicate the hand written letters; the letters in the Typewriter font were typed.

DEDICATION

My name is Ellen Meskimen-Hustad. I am Orlie's youngest child. My dad passed away at the young age of 54, when I was 13 years old.

I transcribed these letters as a gift for my siblings, and gathered information about the war from other sources to help fill in the gaps.

I would like to express sincere gratitude to Jeff Brown from Jackson, Wyoming, for sharing invaluable historical information related to the 133rd Infantry Regiment, 34th "Red Bull" Division's role during World War II. Mr. Brown obtained this information from his grandfather who also served in the division during the war. This information is presented in the shadowed boxes throughout the book. Additional information can be found at www.34thinfantry.com.

The letters were transcribed exactly as my father wrote them. They are the story of a young man who had only known a simple life in his small Iowa town before the war turned him into a soldier and a leader. As a First Sergeant, he managed to survive some truly horrendous battle conditions in Africa and Italy.

During World War II, the 34th Infantry "Red Bull" Division, as part of the United States North African invasion force, was credited as having the first American soldier to step off the boat in support of the war effort on North African soil. The 34th Division holds the distinction of having spent more days in combat than any other US Army Division in World War II, as well as having taken more enemy-defended hills than any other. The Division's casualties totaled 21,362 killed, wounded or missing. These are horrendous statistics, and casualties of the 34th Division are considered to be the highest of any division in the theater when daily per capita fighting strengths are considered.

My memories of my dad are from a 13-year old's perspective. I remember my dad as possessing a quiet strength and being extremely funny. He was a good dad. He was special. And although my memories are not as vivid as I would like them to be, I know that he loved me very much. I miss him.

This is my love letter to my dad.

Dear folks,
~~Love~~ Orlie

MARCH 1941
CAMP CLAIBORNE, LOUISIANA

March 1, 1941 – Arrived at Camp Claiborne for intensive training

Camp Claiborne, Alexandria, LA

March 3, 1941

Dear Folks,

Well, we got here at noon today. The weather is simply grand here. We run around in shirt sleeves. The camp is very modern. Hot and cold running water, swell tents, good beds, fine food, etc. I'll write a letter when I get a little more time.

Love,
Orlie

Orlie Meskimen

▼

Camp Claiborne, Alexandria, LA

March 6, 1941

Dear Folks,

Well, here it is Thursday. It's raining a little today. However, the weather has been fine. I wish you would send my watch down to me. I really need it. I'll write a letter Sunday when I have more time. Send the watch as soon as possible.

Love,
Orlie

Dear Folks, Love Orlie

▼

Camp Claiborne, Alexandria, LA

March 7, 1941

Dear Folks,

    Well, here it is Friday. The weather has changed. It's cold and rainy now. The temperature is about 65, which is low down here.

    The camp (by way of description) covers approximately 3,500 acres. It's located in pine country. The soil is a bright red clay. The main trees are pine, spruce, tamarack and cypress. The cypress trees are very pretty. They have long mossy streamers which reach the ground. Everything is very pretty.

    My duties consist of the following things. I have been picked out for intelligence work. I think I will like it a lot. I will be made a corporal in the next few weeks. Our company will swell to twice its peace time roster in the next two weeks. We (Hq Det) will get approximately 25 drafters. So there has to be some more corporals made to drill them. I am now Senior First Class Private, which means I am next up for promotion.

    Our routine seems to be awfully hard on Tom. Yesterday we went 16 miles through mud and rain in full war pack. I can assure you there were some tired men when we got home.

    I like the fellows in my tent fine. There's Tom, Shadow Williams, Ivo Kelly, Eddie Traber and myself. Traber and myself being in charge. Traber is a corporal and I'm 1st class. Of course, I'm second in command. I like Traber very well. He's exceptionally good. Well I'll write more later. I got a letter from Diane. Sure glad to get it. She surely must be taking it hard.

Well, bye.

Love,
Orlie

Dear Folks, Love Orlie

▼

Camp Claiborne, Alexandria, LA

March 10, 1941

Dear Folks,

    Well, here it is Monday. The weather has changed again for the better. It's very warm out. I'm getting sunburned. My nose is peeling off already.
    Yesterday we paraded before the Governor of Louisiana. It sure was thrilling to see 30,000 soldiers marching. You can't imagine the large amount of space it takes for that many men. The whole 34th Division was finally assembled before the Governor's reviewing stand and he gave a very nice speech welcoming us to Louisiana.
    I think everybody is more or less homesick. You can hardly say anything to anybody they're all so cranky – myself included.
    We took some pictures today. As soon as they're developed I'll send some home. We took pictures of the five of us in our tent, the mess hall, swimming pool, and pictures of each man individually. I hope they are good. Tom hasn't been feeling very good; he's had a headache a lot. I feel fine – better than ever before. I've gained about five pounds.
    The fellows in our tent want to get a small radio. It would cost us about $5 a piece. I wonder if Sam and John would loan it to me until I get my check. We've had one drill check for $5. But it's almost gone. I bought six pairs of underwear, toiletries, etc. I will get a check about the 10th of April for about $47. I could pay Sam and John back then. Ask them as soon as possible. It gets so awfully lonesome at

Orlie Meskimen

night. I guess I miss you folks and Diane too much. Please see them as soon as possible and send me the money if they agree.

Write me often.

Love,
Orlie
XXXXXX
P.S. These letters I write are to all of you.

Dear Folks, Love Orlie

▼

Camp Claiborne, Alexandria, LA

March 21, 1941

Dear Folks,

Well, here I am again! The weather's terrible down here. It's been raining all day and all night last night. The mud is about six inches deep everywhere. It surely is hard to get around. We've started going to school so we won't drill but one hour a day for thirteen weeks. I have been placed as assistant map maker and reader in the intelligence section. I should get a specialist's rating in this section. It's very interesting and should prove valuable in later life. I am learning a little about surveying. It's pretty hard but it comes pretty easy for me because of my college training.

Our regiment will take on 800 drafters in about two weeks which will also mean a lot of advancements. I surely hope I get one. There are five of us up for corporals. Of course, there are three fellows ahead of me. I don't know just how many corporals they will make for sure but I think there will be four. I should be a technical sergeant by the time the year's up. This would be due to my work in the intelligence section.

The weather must be bad there too. It's really nice down here when the sun is out. Everything is the brightest green you ever saw. Of course, there is no vegetation or trees in camp. The earth has had all the sod scraped off. The soil is a bright red clay. I'm going to get some color film one of these days and take some pictures.

I wonder if you folks can send me 75 cents or a dollar

Orlie Meskimen

as soon as possible. I need it for tobacco and stamps. If you have it, will you send it by return mail? I need it so terribly bad. Well, I guess I'll close and go shower. It's 11 o'clock and I'm getting very tired.

Very sincerely,
Orlie
P.S. Write me often. Love.

Dear Folks, Love Orlie

▼

Camp Claiborne, Alexandria, LA

March 31, 1941

Dear Folks,

 I received your latest letter in which the money was enclosed. I'll send it back as soon as I get my check, which should be sometime next week. I'll write a letter soon, before the weekend. I enjoy your letters very much. Tell some of the other folks to write me.

Love,
Orlie

Orlie Meskimen

▼

Camp Claiborne, LA

April 2, 1941

Dear Folks,

Well I'm finally writing you a letter. I've been so busy it's been awfully hard to find time to write. Even Diane says I don't write often enough. She writes me about three times a week and usually more.

I've been having extensive schooling so you see my daylight hours are pretty well taken. At night there's usually a rifle or my pistol to clean for inspection. We have a complete inspection once a week. This covers the tent, equipment and body. I have "short-arm" inspection twice a month.

I weigh about 180 stripped now – it's mostly in my legs and shoulders. I'm getting very brown since the sun is very hot down here now. The temperature ranges between 90 and 100 degrees from 7 in the morning until after 8 o'clock at night. It gets hot early and stays hot until well after dark. However, the nights are cool and swell for sleeping.

I'm listening to Kay Kyser now. We have a nice little radio and get lots of good southern music. We get Des Moines sometimes on a good clear night. It comes in good sometimes. The radio gives us a lot of company. We always listen to the "Hit Parade" on Saturday night. It's about the only program we hear down here that is familiar. We're close enough to Mexico that we hear a lot of Mexican language and music.

By the way, I've been pretty sick. I've been confined to

Dear Folks, Love Orlie

quarters for four days. I had a very sore throat and cough. It's better now though and I feel pretty good. It seems practically everybody's having the same trouble.

I've had some pictures taken and will send them in my next letter. Some of them are pretty funny. They will probably make people all over Shellsburg laugh. I'll wait and let you see for yourselves.

I like the Army better every day and time is beginning to pass very quickly. I won't be able to send any money home until I get my corporal's rating, which should be very soon. We (the 34th Division) are getting 850 drafters and all the men now in will get ratings of some kind. I should think the drafters will cause us a lot of review. But it probably will be fun teaching them what we know.

Tom and I are now classified as troopers or front line troops. That is, if war was declared, we would automatically be moved to the battle front. However, I don't believe the Army expects war. <u>But we do have a very modern Army</u>. More so than any civilian can even realize.

Well, I guess I'll close and go shower. I take a shower every morning and night.

Bye.

Love,
Orlie
XXXXX

Orlie Meskimen

▼

Camp Claiborne, LA

April 6, 1941

Dear Folks,

I just got back from Baton Rouge. I have enclosed some comical pictures. I hope you enjoy them. I am going to shower now so I'll close and write you later. I'll send some more pictures later. Write me often. I enjoy your letters a lot.

Love,
Orlie
P.S. I'm sending Diane identical pictures.

▼

Camp Claiborne, LA

April 8, 1941

Dear Folks,

I am sending some more pictures. I hope you enjoy them. Some of the fellows you won't know but keep the pictures because I will want them when the year is up. I plan on coming home on a leave sometime in July. It's getting hotter down here every day. However, the sun does seem good.

Love,
Orlie

Dear Folks, Love Orlie

▼

Camp Claiborne, LA

April 9, 1941

Dear Folks,

Here are a couple more pictures of me. The one gives the impression of me drinking. But we weren't – it was all in fun. The other shows me (the tall fellow with his back turned in the foreground) leaving the road for a rest period during a march. It shows some of the mud and water so evident at that time. It doesn't resemble me but I think it was the light at that time.

The weather is very warm now and the air is continually hot and moist. I don't believe it will bother me though – it hasn't yet. Today we saw an engineer's exhibition. We saw them throw a 264 foot pontoon bridge across the Red River in eight minutes. Then we all had to run across it with full pack. It swayed and dipped so much you could hardly stay on it. This man's Army is rapidly developing into an extremely fast mechanized Army which could move from 30 to 100 miles a day against stiff gunfire. I believe we would be ready at any time should the situation present itself.

I haven't heard from you folks for two days. What's the matter? Are you slipping? I enjoy getting letters. Sometimes I'm a little slow in writing but it's because I'm either tired or busy, so don't worry. I'm getting along just fine. I get letters from you folks, Diane, Junior, Bunky, Clare, and I sent Verna Dickson a card tonight so I'll probably hear from her too. I get a letter every day and I surely enjoy them.

I hope your operation was a success, mother. But

where were the tumors? I couldn't get that part from your card.

I saw the .50 caliber machine gun fired yesterday. It will shoot through 1-3/4 inches of steel armor plate, which is heavy enough for the heaviest tanks used anywhere. Well, I'll close and write later.

Love,
Orlie
XXXXXXXXX

Dear Folks, Love Orlie

▼

Camp Claiborne, LA

April 12, 1941

Dear Folks,

Here are two more pictures of me, one with one of my buddies. He's from Cedar Rapids and a very nice fellow. Both pictures were taken at Baton Rouge last Sunday. The palm trees in the picture are small but were as big as the camera would take. Baton Rouge has a population of 150,000, and is beyond doubt the prettiest town I've every seen. The state university and capital are both there.

I've sent Diane various pictures so when she comes up you may compare them. I surely miss her. I guess she misses me quite a lot too, although I've heard rumors she has been stepping out. If I were sure I would quit writing her. If I found out she was I think I would stay in the Army. You see I can stay here five years and by that time I should be fairly high and could transfer into another barracks or camp. I may stay anyway if the set-up looks promising. She seems to think it would be fun. I'm planning on coming home in July because I can get a ten day leave at that time. At that rate I could be home about a week. All the fellows will get two ten-day leaves this year but they must be taken separately.

I wish you would get more people to write me because the life down here is getting steadily tougher. The hikes are terrible. You carry a full pack (110 pounds) and go 20 to 30 miles. I've saw scores of fellows coming back in ambulances. Also I've saw fellows who were crazy enough to march along bleeding at the nose. So far I've gotten along fine outside of the big toe I smashed on the section last summer. I have an ingrown toenail which will be operated on Monday. I surely hope the medics can help it. It gets almost unbearable at times on the march. We are on wartime rations now so we're not overfed. However, I'm steadily gaining weight. I weigh 185 stripped now which is heavier than I've ever been before.

Well, I'll close now and mail this bit of nonsense. Well, so long for now.

Love,
Orlie

Dear Folks, Love Orlie

▼

Camp Claiborne, LA

April 16, 1941

Dear Folks,

Well, here it is Wednesday and a very nice day. The weather has been very pleasant down here. The nights are so cool you have to sleep with a comforter and wool blanket over you. The days are pretty warm. Its been up over 100 degrees already. It promises to get very hot though yet.

We go to Texas for six weeks of wartime maneuvers sometime before long. We're going on the dessert – I guess they figure when a man's been on the dessert in strenuous exercise for that long he's capable of putting up a scrap wherever the actual wartime battle front may be.

I'm getting heavier and harder every day. You will surely be surprised when you see me. I'll bet my civilian clothes at home won't fit me now. I'm beginning to get into the groove more each day. Whenever I hear a band or see a flag chills run up my spine. You get the feeling you would sacrifice your life gladly than see the colors in another country's hands. That may sound silly but it eventually comes into every soldier's heart.

I'm sending some pictures of various scenes in Baton Rouge. Keep all these pictures. I got your pictures and they were very good. Jeepy surely looked cute. He seemed to be fatter. Well I'll close and mail this in the morning.

Love,
Orlie

Orlie Meskimen

▼

Camp Claiborne, LA

April 20, 1941

Dear Folks,

Well, how are all you folks by now? I'm fine. They haven't operated on my toe yet but I expect they will soon because its gotten pretty sore. The medics are so busy you just have to wait until they can get to you. Have you received all the pictures I sent you? I hope you enjoy them. I will send some more later on. I am thinking of having a large portrait taken for Diane – she wants one so bad. I got a very nice letter from her today. I get about three letters a week from her. I got your latest letter also the letter Diane sent you. It was a nice letter. I guess she does think quite a lot of me. I surely am in love with her. I guess I didn't realize how much until I came down here. She's been planning on our living in a trailer house. I guess it would work until I could get us on our feet. I figure if I make a Sergeant by mid-summer we could get along pretty good. She's awfully sweet and I love her so much. I guess that's enough of that foolish babble.

It's raining down here tonight. It's the first rain we've had for about two weeks. It was getting pretty dry. The weather down here has been grand. However, everything else is terrible. Please don't tell Diane how things actually are because she would probably worry a lot. I paint the picture pretty rosy for her benefit. Someday I'll tell her just how things were when we're together. We have everything planned for our future. I only hope something doesn't ruin

Dear Folks, Love Orlie

all our plans. I really don't believe we will ever go to war. However, things are pretty complicated over across the water now. But the English seem to be doing pretty good now. I notice they are driving the Germans back in places. I hope they continue to whip them. Well, I'll close and write some more tomorrow.

    Well, here it is Sunday and a very nice day. It has stopped raining and the sun is shining very brightly. The ground can be mud four inches deep as it was last night and dry out completely in a few hours when the sun shines. The soil is clay and drains very quickly. It gets almost unbearably hot in the afternoons and like all true southerners the Army is gradually swinging the groove of having a siesta time in the afternoon. We're all gradually getting lazier. There's something about the southern weather that gets you so you're tired all the time. It makes no difference how much sleep one gets at night, he's still tired. Some fellow is playing an accordion down the line and it sounds pretty good. Well, I guess I'll close for now and write again later.

Write often.
Love,
Orlie

Orlie Meskimen

▼

Camp Claiborne, LA

April 23, 1941

Dear Folks,

Well here it is Wednesday night and it's raining. It has been raining for the past two days and nights. It's a cold rain and makes everyone very miserable.

We got sixteen drafters today from Minnesota and they all seem to be nice fellows. Most of them are pretty green and have an awful lot to learn. But we got the cream of the crop so I guess they will soon learn. I hear Porter A, Bill Coy and Orville S. all may have to go. I surely hope they take Porter. They will either make a man of him or kill him. Take it from me – I know. Porter would have a terrible time taking orders.

I am sending some small pictures of a bridge that Tom, Corporal Emery and I are making. Have I sent a picture of Corporal Emery home? Please tell me because he's Tom's and my buddy. He's really a swell fellow. We are beginning to be called the Three Musketeers. Most of the fellows either call me Doug or "Mac". There are two Meskimen's in Camp Claiborne. It's a father and his son. The old fellow's name is Dave. I'm going to look them up some day. I've heard this Dave is even bigger than I am. Maybe they are some of our relations. I'll finish this in ink and mail it right away.

Love,
Orlie

Dear Folks, Love Orlie

Camp Claiborne, LA

April 30, 1941

Dear Folks,

Just a line to let you know I'm alright. But Tom was sent to the hospital this morning with measles. Our company has been on the rifle range so far this week and will continue to be for the remainder of this week and all of next. It has been raining down here the past two days but looks as though it might clear up soon. I surely hope so. Has Diane been up to see you? Write her a letter, why don't you? I'm sure she would enjoy it.

Love,
Orlie

Orlie Meskimen

▼

Camp Claiborne, LA

May 5, 1941

Dear Folks,

Well, here it is Monday and we've had a terrible storm all last night and all day today. We had a 60 MPH gale in from the gulf. It's been raining very hard and everything is a veritable mass of mud. The tents are tracked up so bad it will take a week to clean them out.

I am sending a picture. I'm not sure maybe I've sent one like it. I've numbered each man so you can tell who the boys are. 2nd Lieutenant Elliot is now the commanding officer of our unit and is young and a very nice fellow. He's just 26 years old. First Sergeant Blanik is our Detachment First Sergeant. He also is a good fellow. He's married and has three children. Sergeant Priborsky is a Staff Sergeant and has charge of the message center section and also the drill of the detachment. Lyman Emery isn't with us anymore – he transferred to cooks and bakers school at Fort Benning, Georgia.

By the way, I think perhaps I'll transfer to an engineering company after maneuvers. By then I should be a technical sergeant and could maybe make a 2nd Louie in an engineering outfit. Practically every old man will leave here a non-com. Tom should be a corporal by the time the year's out. Tom tries very hard and is certainly a changed fellow. We have a bunch of ratings coming up soon and I know I will be a Corporal. They are begging for officers here now and have very little old experienced material from which to

Dear Folks, Love Orlie

draw them. So the young men who are earnestly trying are getting the ratings.

Well, folks, I'm not very good at writing but I try to let you know I'm alive. Oh yes, I've had two very sweet letters from Diane so don't worry about us. She said she was going to visit you soon. I'm glad to hear everything looks so nice. I think I will be home in the early part of June to see it. If I don't get home in June I'll be home in August. That will be after maneuvers. Well, I'll close for now and write more later.

Love,
Orlie

Orlie Meskimen

▼

Camp Claiborne, LA

May 9, 1941

Dear Folks,

    Well, here it is Friday and it's pretty hot – the temperature is around 100 degrees. We take concentrated sodium chloride tablets in order to keep enough salt in our systems. Otherwise I don't believe a fellow could stand it. I am sending home a picture of a soldier who didn't make the grade – save it for me. I sent Diane a large picture of the camp. She will bring it up when she comes. I get a letter from her nearly every day. The reason I didn't hear from her before was because she didn't have a stamp. She couldn't get out during the day and when evening came the post office was closed.

    I hope you folks enjoy the telegrams and the cards. I am going to wire you folks Sunday. I hope the telegram doesn't frighten you. It's so hard to mail a box from here or I would have sent you a present. However, I tried to make the sentiments nice. Diane sent me some snap shots and she looks heavier. Gosh, I'm getting as black as a negro. I weigh 185 stripped. Most of it is in my arms and shoulders. My face is full now too. I had my toe fixed. They just froze it and lifted the nail up. Also I have had two teeth pulled and some fillings put in. They put in a gold filling where I had the porcelain. So, my teeth are in good shape. I spent a dollar in town and

Dear Folks, Love Orlie

had them cleaned. Well, I guess I'll close now. I'm afraid I'm a poor writer.

Love, Orlie

P.S. You don't need to send me comic strips because we get the Gazette down here. It sure seems good.

Camp Claiborne, LA

May 13, 1941

Dear Folks,

I received your letter and was glad you like the telegrams. I want you to find out Spurgeon's address and let me know. I'll look him up because I know he would be glad to see anyone from home. I know he could be in this camp and we'd never see him unless we looked for him. Write.

Love,
Orlie

Orlie Meskimen

Camp Claiborne, LA

May 21, 1941

Dear Folks,

Well, how are you? I am fine in spite of the terrible heat down here. It gets so hot in the day time it's almost unbearable. We have finished all our range work now until after the big maneuvers in September. I have fired 300 rounds. That is – 100 rounds each for the 1903 Springfield rifle, the Garand M1, and the .45 Colt revolver. This new Garand is one of the smoothest firing pieces I've ever seen. It reloads faster than one can pull the trigger. The slide mechanism works so fast the firer can't see it go. I have also seen the .30 and .50 caliber machine guns, and the .61 and .80 millimeter trench mortars in action. Also we can hear heavy artillery both day and night. Now that the range work is over I guess we'll go to school for 32 days. The rumor is that we won't get leaves until after maneuvers – General Marshall's orders. It must be the present condition abroad. Please don't tell Diane – it would only worry her. I got the letter she sent you, it was a nice letter. She said she was looking forward to seeing you folks but just hasn't been able to arrange it yet. She's terribly afraid you will be mad. I wish I could arrange to get her down here for a week or so

Dear Folks, Love Orlie

– but people would probably talk a lot and it might hurt her reputation. If the order on leaves does go through it would mean I couldn't get home until about October. When I get my next stripes maybe we can get married – although the climate might be too severe for her down here. Have you read much about the 4th Army maneuvers? You see, we have four Army's and I belong to the 4th. I guess we are going to maneuver right here in Louisiana. Well, I guess I'd better close and mail this – it's almost time for evening mess.

Love,
Orlie

Orlie Meskimen

▼

Camp Claiborne, LA

May 28, 1941

Dear Folks,

Just a line to let you know I'm still alive. It has been raining down here today but I guess it's all over now. How is everything in Shellsburg? Still the same old burg? I suppose the same as usual. I suppose Jack will soon be in the Army. What does Aunt Mabel and Jack think about it? I don't suppose Jack is looking forward to coming. I think this camp is full now unless the camp is enlarged more.

Love,
Orlie

Dear Folks, Love Orlie

▼

Camp Claiborne, LA

May 31, 1941

Dear Folks,

Well, it's Saturday night and I'm on C.Q. (charge of quarters). In this job the man selected must watch the company street, all the tents, and answer the office telephone occasionally. It really isn't as difficult as it may sound.

It has been raining the past week almost consistently. Not a hard rain but an almost ever persisting patter. I am in the company office now listening to the Hit Parade. Remember how I used to like to listen to it back home? I like the songs "My Sister and I," "The Things I Love," and "Taps Till Reveille." Have you heard them? I like the last one especially well. It always makes me think of Diane. I guess she must miss me a lot – she wants to come down if I don't get to come home but I'm afraid people would talk. I'd surely like to have her come though anyway.

Could you see my tent in the large picture Diane left for you? I have a circle drawn around it. I'll explain all about it when I come home.

I received a letter from Aunt Mabel. Also I dropped Oscar a card about three days ago. I enjoy getting letters quite a bit. I got a letter from Lucille Steger (Chittick). I don't know where she obtained my address but I guess she didn't mean anything. It was a nice friendly letter, she said she knows I must be sort of blue down here and since we used to be such good friends she thought she should write me.

Orlie Meskimen

We're pretty inactive down here now. But I guess maneuvers will give us plenty to do. There is a lot of talk of holding us over a year. I don't know whether there's much to it or not. Diane worries so much about such things. I don't believe they will hold us long after the war abroad is over. Well, I guess I'd better close. Write.

Love,
Orlie
XXXX

Dear Folks, Love Orlie

▼

Camp Claiborne, LA

June 6, 1941

Dear Folks,

How are you? I'm fine or as well as could be expected. Will you please send me my book on trigonometry and college algebra. I want to use them to pass the evenings. I'll write a long letter this weekend. I received your most recent letter yesterday.

Love,
Orlie

Orlie Meskimen

Camp Claiborne, LA

June 7, 1941

Dear Folks,

Just a line to let you know I'm still alive and well. It's raining awfully hard this afternoon. It always does rain on weekends when we're on our own time. It has been pretty hot all week so this rain is pretty welcome as far as the temperature goes. I talked to a native who said it wasn't hot yet and still the soldiers think it's terrible. It has run right around 100 so far this week. The air is sort of hot and sticky due mainly to the excessive amounts of moisture in the air. Our clothes are damp every morning when we get up. The nights are positively grand, however, cool and awfully bright. I have had four letters from Diane this week. Roosevelt's speech disturbs her quite a bit. I really didn't see anything in it to get alarmed about but she seems to be scared to death. She has written me four twelve-page letters so you can see she's worrying. Personally I don't think Hitler wants any trouble with a country as strong as America. If you could see a full American armored division rolling across the country you would understand how really hard it would be to stop the penetrating power of such a division. I am going to get pictures of tanks, command cars, jeeps, trucks, weapon carriers, etc. and send them home soon.

Dear Folks, Love Orlie

We hear the news from Des Moines nearly every night. It comes in good on a clear night. None of the Chicago stations come in though. Our best stations are Memphis, New Orleans, Alexandria, St. Louis and the Texas stations.

Well, it's Monday and I guess I'd better get this letter away. I was busy yesterday and didn't get to finish this letter then so I'm doing it now. I guess I'd better get ready to go to work so I'll close now.

Love,
Orlie

P.S. Here's a terrible picture of me. I need a shave.

Orlie Meskimen

▼

Camp Claiborne, LA

June 16, 1941

Dear Folks,

Well, it's raining again today so I've a little time to write. I'm sending a picture of a new selectee and myself. Quite a contrast, don't you think? The last picture I sent you was taken just after we had come in from an all night hike. I was dead tired and needed a shave pretty bad. I guess it wasn't such a bad picture though!

We're going on another all night hike tonight in spite of the rain. We aren't allowed to either talk or smoke. Airplanes drove over head all the time and keep dropping flares trying to locate us. You see, they represent simulated enemy planes trying to strike the infantry ranks on the ground. Sometimes they locate us and drive down within 50 feet of our heads, their machine guns blasting away. Of course, they are shooting blanks. But you find yourself taking cover just as frantically as if it were all real.

How is everything at home? I suppose the weather is nice up there now. It rains a lot down here but it's very welcome because when the sun comes out the heat is <u>sweltering</u>. If I pull through the heat down here I'll never have

Dear Folks, Love Orlie

to worry about it anywhere else. I'm sorry, dad, to hear you have a carbunckle – it must be pretty painful. I hope you enjoyed the card.

    I received the books – I plan on going to night school soon. They are going to open schools in mathematics and foreign language. I guess I'll study German. Well, I guess I'd better close. It's so awfully hard to find much to write.

Love,
Orlie

Orlie Meskimen

▼

Camp Claiborne, LA

June 26, 1941

Dear Folks,

 I'm sorry I haven't written sooner but we have been out on maneuvers since last Thursday so I haven't had time to write much. We are going back in Friday night so I will write a letter this weekend. I received your last letter and was glad to hear Dad's neck is better. It must have been awfully sore. Well, I guess I'd better close for this time.

Love,
Orlie

Dear Folks, Love Orlie

▼

Camp Claiborne, LA

June 28, 1941

Dear Folks,

    Well, I'm home again from maneuvers and I'm surely glad to be here. We put in eight of the darndest days I've ever seen. It rained almost consistently and we were awake almost all the time. Probably you've read about it. Our regiment whipped the enemy. Our regiment (133rd – 538 men) whipped two divisions (32nd & 37th – 20,000 men). Colonel Greenfield, our field marshal, is one of the best tacticians the Army has today, and the 133rd is the best regiment in all four Army's. During the maneuvers I counted eight times I would have been killed if it had been actual war. But all these things teach a fellow what could happen if we were in war. We will go out for two weeks starting the 11th of August, then come in for two days and go out again for four weeks – that will surely be a grind.

    You can expect me home in July. I will wire Diane and she can meet me with you up home. The woman she works for told her she can have a vacation anytime I come home. I surely need a rest, they've darn near worked us to death the past few weeks. I've lost weight until I just weigh 170 now. But I'm still heavier than I was when last you saw me.

    Homer Woodson was over awhile last night. I guess he hates the Army pretty bad. I suppose he misses Louise Dice a lot. He has lost a lot of weight. They have been feeding us good lately but it's so hot and we're so active we sweat it out. Also our tans are fading, I guess we're sweating them out too.

I suppose you know George King is home. Since he was the company clerk he rated the first leave. I guess Tom and I won't be able to come together because I'm higher on the merit system than he is.

I am glad Russia is fighting Germany. Maybe it will turn the tide of the war in England's favor. I guess Russia has stopped the German advance in several places. I hope they are able to give the Germans a heck of a fight.

Here is a sticker which came attached to a package of gum and cigarettes they sent to all the boys from Cedar Rapids and vicinity. Well, I guess I'd better close for now. Put this sticker in my scrapbook.

Love,
Orlie

Dear Folks, Love Orlie

Camp Claiborne, LA

July 12, 1941

Dear Folks,

I received your nice letter this morning and was awfully glad to get it. It has been raining here for two days and so things are pretty dreary.

I guess my leave will start the 15th of this month. Wish I could come home but I guess it's impossible because I can't get the money together. I tried to get my money from the finance company I have it invested with but they wouldn't let me have it because my contract calls for the first of October. Lieutenant Thill, my company commander, even offered to sign for me but they wouldn't let me have it. I don't know how to tell Diane I won't be home until nearly the first of November. I know she will feel as bad as I do and probably worse. I wouldn't mind it so much if it weren't for the big maneuvers that start the 15th of August and end September 21st. That will surely be a grind. I guess we will all be checked physically before we go but I know I'll be in good enough shape to be selected to go. Most of the fighting will be on the dessert. I'm sort of afraid of the heat – I've been sick several times because of it already. It gets much hotter down here than in Iowa. They are issuing concentrated salt tablets now but they don't seem to do much good.

I suppose Jack is happy because he won't have to go. He'll never know how lucky he is to be able to stay home. You can't find a fellow down here who doesn't want to be home. They aren't feeding us very good now for the long hours we put in on these maneuvers. Maybe things will be better this fall after the big maneuvers are over. Most of us are eating down at the canteen during the evenings so we aren't starving, but it costs a lot. Well, I guess I'd better close for now. Drop Diane a letter occasionally – she worries quite a lot.

Love,
Orlie
P.S. I'm glad Dad is feeling better and is able to be around again.

Dear Folks, Love Orlie

▼

Camp Claiborne, LA

July 20, 1941

Dear Folks,

I thought I would write you a few lines tonight. It's been a pretty nice day down here today. I've been swimming all day and so I feel a little tired tonight. I am enclosing a picture from the Southern Military Review which was taken when we passed in review on the 4th of July. This is Hq. Det. with all its officers. The officers are the fellows in front saluting. I have a circle drawn around my head so you could see me. We're going to have some of these pictures made and I will send you one you can see better. The officer in the extreme lower left hand corner is Lieutenant W. Kansky who served in France with Burley. He used to be a cop in Cedar Rapids before the guards were mobilized. The officers on the reviewing stand are Lieutenant, Brigade, Major and Four Star Generals. It took five hours for the 34th Division to pass the stand – a total of about 25,000 men. This, of course, includes Infantry, Artillery, Medics, Engineers, Heavy Weapons companies and Panzer Units. There are three such divisions here within a radius of 60 miles – Claiborne (34), Livingston (32), and Beauregard (37). Also Camp Polk is about 80 miles away so you can see Louisiana has her share of troops.

The southerners sometimes become very insulting. The older generation still holds the Civil War against us. The young men hate us too because lots of them are losing their girls and everywhere they go is jammed with soldiers. Company L from Dubuque has been confined to their company street because one of their boys was killed in town by six cab drivers. I guess they were preparing to administer a similar fate to the drivers. They were armed with scissors, Bolo knives (a Bolo knife is a trench weapon), and bayonets. The cab drivers beat this soldier to death with jack handles.

If you will notice in the picture the average soldier is taller than six foot. Of course, there are some shorter but they must be in almost perfect physical condition. Well, I guess I'd better close. Bye.

Orlie
XXXX
P.S. Write me.

Dear Folks, Love Orlie

▼

Camp Claiborne, LA

July 23, 1941

Dear Folks,

I received both of your most recent letters okay and was glad to get them. I am sending along a few pictures which I want you to save for me. How is everything at home? I suppose everything is about the same. The heat is not so bad down here now. We have had considerable amounts of rain during the last week or so! Write.

Love,
Orlie

Orlie Meskimen

▼

Camp Claiborne, LA

July 27, 1941

Dear Folks,

Well, how are you by this time? I am fine or as well as could be expected with all this heat. The heat has been intense the past two weeks. But it's rather cool today because we had a rain last night.

You wanted to know about the trip we took so here goes. We went through Texas down to Beaumont and Port Arthur. Both are gulf ports and very pretty towns. Beaumont is an oil town and Port Arthur is one of the largest port towns on the gulf. It was a very nice trip and we enjoyed ourselves a lot. The temperature down there was exceedingly cool because of the tide coming in. You see nothing but palm and magnolia trees down there and practically everyone runs around in shorts. The gulf was a disappointment though – it was so muddy you couldn't see three inches down in it. But I guess that was because of the tide coming in.

I believe Germany is finally stalemated in her war with Russia. She attacked Russia for two main reasons: wheat and oil and so far she has obtained neither. Four weeks ago she attacked to secure the Ukraine wheat region. She attacked then because the wheat was green and she figured Russia would be unable to burn the wheat as she retreated. However, Germany is still being held on the extreme edge of the Ukraine region and during the four weeks the wheat has ripened and the Russians are cutting it and trucking it back into Russia far behind the main line of resistance. What they

Dear Folks, Love Orlie

can't convoy back they can now burn in the case of a major German "push". Hitler has finally reached the end of his rope I believe. I surely hope so because the sooner he does the sooner they will turn us loose.

    I get lots of letters from Diane lately. I got five this week. It begins to look like it will be October before they issue us any more passes or furloughs. I wish I could have come home before maneuvers.

    I actually believe I could get a discharge because of the heat. I get severe headaches which last for days at a time. Nothing I take seems to help in the least. Whether a discharge would be advisable or not I don't know. I've a good notion to try and see what it gains me. I've a good notion to go up this afternoon and at least see if the medics can help me. Well, guess I'd better close for this time.

Love, Orlie XXX

Orlie Meskimen

▼

Camp Claiborne, LA

July 31, 1941

Dear Folks,

I received your box and last letter yesterday. Thanks a million for the box – everything surely tasted good. We don't get much sweet stuff. Please don't buy those things though – I know they must have cost quite a little.

We have been on the "alert" since yesterday morning. Today we had to move the whole division out of camp just to see how rapidly we could move. In three hours we had all moved (23,000 men), all our equipment and were set up ready to do battle ten miles from camp. We had to move the orderly tents, supply tents, kitchens and just everything we have here in camp.

There is considerable talk of us leaving this camp entirely right after maneuvers. That would be about the last of October. They say we will either move to Washington state or New Jersey. I hope we don't move at all even though I hate Louisiana. More than likely we will have to stay more than a year and I'd sooner finish my hitch all in the same place.

There is a lot of talk also about paying us a bonus if they decide to hold us over a year. If some such arrangement isn't made they will have a lot of trouble because lots of the fellows are ready to go over the hill now. It seems everyone here in Claiborne hates the Army so much they would do most anything to get away. I, myself, hate the Army so much I would give most anything to be able to come home. You see, the regular Army has so many more privileges

Dear Folks, Love Orlie

than we of the National Guard. I am a Guardsman now, only instead of being in state service I am in federal service.

Those two Meskimen's I spoke about earlier are from Waterloo. It's a father and his son and both are sergeant's. The father is a mess sergeant and his name is Dave, and the son's name is Frank. They know dad and have visited us a few times. They don't seem to be very well liked in their company though.

Well, I guess I'll close for this time. We leave for six weeks of maneuvers August 12.

Love,
Orlie

> Aug. 11 - Oct. 1, 1941: Participated in Louisiana Maneuvers

Orlie Meskimen

▼

Camp Claiborne, LA

August 11, 1941

Dear Folks,

    I'm leaving on a fifteen day maneuver, so if you don't hear much from me you will understand why. I received your boxes – also Ida's. Thanks a lot! Tell Ida I surely appreciated the cookies and they were very good. I would drop her a card but I don't have time. I guess I'd better get on with my packing.

Love,
Orlie

Dear Folks, Love Orlie

▼

Out on maneuvers

August 13, 1941

Dear Folks,

    Well, we are finally launched on our big six weeks maneuver. We came out Tuesday morning and are now about thirty miles from the Texas border. We will battle here for about two weeks and then move into Texas for four weeks of it. This first fifteen days is a corps area maneuver and the thirty days will be a battle between the 2nd and 3rd armies. There are 250,000 men out here now and after the first of the month there will be more than 500,000. It will be pretty hard work but should be lots of fun anyway.

    I won't have much time to write but I'm enclosing a few more pictures. I have about twice this many but I will have to wait until the next time I write to send the rest of them. Write me often and take care of yourselves.

Love,
Orlie

Orlie Meskimen

▼

Out on maneuvers

August 20, 1941

Dear Folks,

Received your nice letter today and was very glad to hear from you. Mail service is pretty bad and I just received your letter today – 20th. These maneuvers aren't as bad as I figured they would be. We will be out here all of next month I guess so it will be quite a while before we will be back in Claiborne. I'll try to write as often as I possibly can, but it's hard to find time to write. How is everything in Shellsburg? I hear Kate Bergen is pretty sick – is she?

Love,
Orlie

▼

Out on maneuvers

August 26, 1941

Dear Folks,

Well, here it is Monday and, of course, we are still on maneuvers. We have been in camp area reserve for the past few days. I would have written a letter but my stamps and envelopes were all stuck together. How is everything at home? If I get a furlough right after maneuvers it should be time to take Jeepy hunting. I'll bet he will enjoy that. I get a bang just looking at his picture. I'll send you some more pictures soon.

Love, Orlie

Dear Folks, Love Orlie

Out on maneuvers

August 28, 1941

Dear Folks,

Received your letter this morning and was glad to hear from you. I also got one from Diane and one from Louise M. Louise wrote me an awful nice letter. Will you please send me a book of 3 cent stamps. I can't seem to get any out here on maneuvers. I think you can get a book for 37 cents. I'll write you a long letter as soon as I hear from you. Elmer must have a pretty good job now.

Love, Orlie

Out on maneuvers

September 2, 1941

Dear Folks,

Well, here I am writing you a card again. I received your card and also the box Clare sent. I wrote him a letter thanking him. I enjoyed everything very much. Boxes come in even more often on maneuvers than when we're in camp. It's rather cool this morning because it rained last night and it's still cloudy this morning. Well, I'll try to write you a letter soon.

Love,
Orlie

Orlie Meskimen

▼

Out on maneuvers

September 6, 1941

Dear Folks,

I received your letter along with the stamps just now and was very glad to hear from you. The stamps will come in very handy because we are unable to secure them in the field.

Maneuvers are running smoothly because the temperature is cooling off considerably now. Whenever the paper's say anything about them, we are the "Blue Army" so you will know whether or not we are winning. Last night we concluded a huge battle which we won. Today and tomorrow we are on reserve for behind the lines. We are being supported by three large armored divisions. Our outfit, the 1st Battalion of the 133rd, is known as a "blitz" battalion – I'll send you some clippings soon. They are behind the lines in a [illegible] area. I'll be able to tell you much more when I come home.

I'll be glad to be able to go hunting when I come home. I expect Jeepy will enjoy it too. It might be a good plan to oil both guns up in good shape so the mechanism will be in good working order.

By the way, I've been put in charge of the ammunition for the battalion. It means I should have a promotion. Don't say much about it until I'm actually made. I'll tell you all about it when I get home.

Well, I guess I'd better close for this time. I'll see you all soon.

Love, Orlie

Dear Folks, Love Orlie

▼

Out on maneuvers

September 17, 1941

Dear Folks,

Well, here it is Wednesday and we are still on maneuvers. But I guess they will all be over by Monday or Tuesday. I will surely be glad to be through with them.

I have some rather bad news for you and also for myself. Diane sent my ring back about three days ago. Also a letter explaining why, in which she said she was afraid it was all a mistake. Please don't be too quick to criticize her. I understand all her motives and after all, I know her probably better than anyone else. We're going to have a heart to heart talk about it when I come home and will decide upon our final decision at that time. Please don't worry about it – I'm not. Also don't say anything around town until a clean break is definitely made.

I have been sick for two days – had cramps, aching bones and the shits. And when I say the shits I mean the shits! In 26 hours my bowels moved 24 times. Tom is in the same shape. It was caused either by something we ate or the drinking water. You see, all our water is pumped from ponds and creeks and purified with iodine. It's hot and putrid tasting.

We have seen everything our Army has to offer in the way of equipment now. I'll tell you all about it when I come home. This is rather short but we're going back to the front and I'll have to rush away. Here are some pictures.

Love, Orlie

Orlie Meskimen

▼

Out on maneuvers

September 20, 1941

Dear Folks,

I have a few more pictures to send you so I thought I would write a few lines along with them. Most of them you already have but I'm ruining them by carrying them with me.

Well, I'm all over my sickness now and feel a lot better. Lots of fellows are just coming down with it – I sure pity them. I'm still a little weak but gaining strength every day. I've lost about ten pounds in maneuvers but that's natural because of the strenuous exercise. But they will be over soon now so I guess I've really nothing to kick about.

I haven't written back to Clare yet but will as soon as I finish this letter. He sent me two dollars in his letter which should come in handy.

These maneuvers so far have killed 225 men – 250 were estimated to be killed. That's really not so many considering that there are 550,000 out here and all the night rides we take at break-neck speed.

You will have to excuse my writing but I only have an old board to write on.

Love, Orlie

Dear Folks, Love Orlie

▼

Camp Claiborne, LA

September 29, 1941

Dear Folks,

Just a line to let you know maneuvers are over and we are back in Camp Claiborne. They ended at 4:25 Sunday afternoon. I'm surely glad they are over – we were all getting so tired of them.

I am enclosing a few more pictures – some I had laid away and forgotten. Some of them are nearly ruined.

From all word so far received I will be home on the 12th of the month. Maybe we will only get twelve days but I hope for more.

Well, I guess I'd better close. Tell Clare I was glad to hear from him and hope he is soon feeling better.

Bye,
Orlie

Orlie Meskimen

▼

Camp Claiborne, LA

October 3, 1941

Dear Folks,

Well, here it is Friday and we have the day off. The reason being that we took lock-jaw shots this morning and we're all a little woozy. There have been several cases in the past two weeks and they are trying to stop the spread. Most of them are from severe chigger bites.

I am sending a few more pictures. Maybe I can get most of them home before I come so it will be easier. I'll have a lot of things to carry as it is.

You can expect me home anytime now. Not later than the 15th. Probably the 12th will be the day I'll arrive. But I'm definitely coming home very soon.

I had my first date since I left last February last night. The girl's name is Bette Panda and she's awfully nice. She's about 5'8", weighs about 130, and has coal black hair and sort of olive complexion. She's French and really shows it. I'll bring her picture when I come home.

Well, guess I'd better close now. It's raining here today.

Love,
Orlie
P.S. I'll definitely be home between the 11th and 15th. Word just came through. Tom will be there too.

Dear Folks, Love Orlie

Mid to Late October – Furlough

▼

Camp Claiborne, LA

October 29, 1941

Dear Folks,

Arrived in camp in good time so I'll write you a few lines. We had rather bad weather all the way down. It rained a lot but in spite of it we made it about as we figured we would. The Ozarks were very pretty but due to rain and cloudy weather I'm afraid our pictures will be no good. I suppose it still rains up there. It's rather cool down here and cloudy today but I doubt if this weather will continue for any length of time. Write.

Love,
Orlie

Orlie Meskimen

Camp Claiborne, LA

October 29, 1941

Dear Folks,

    Well, I'm all settled so I'll write a few lines. We got here Tuesday at about 10 o'clock in the morning without any trouble. We took plenty of time coming back and enjoyed ourselves a lot.

    So far since I've been back I have been coaching on the rifle range. It's tiresome work and aggravating at times but isn't really hard work. All I have to do is check the firers for trigger squeeze, flinching, and other faults that cause defective firing. Of course, if I discover these faults it's my job to correct them. But I guess you'd rather not hear about such things especially since probably you don't understand them.

    Everything is pretty much the same in camp. Everyone was glad to see us and we were pretty glad to see them. The weather is rather cool here now but still warm enough to go without a shirt. It rained a little last night but not enough to get muddy.

    I had a very nice letter from LaVonne B. today. She surely hated to see me come back last Sunday night. I had quite a time getting away from her. Also, she sent me a nice picture. It's pretty good sized – about 6 x 8 and in natural color.

    Well, I guess I'd better close for this time. I'll write more later. Write when you can.

Love, Orlie

Dear Folks, Love Orlie

▼

Camp Claiborne, LA

November 10, 1941

Dear Folks,

    Well, how are you? I'm fine or as well as could be expected. Say, I wonder if dad could send me the shotgun sometime soon? The duck hunting is pretty good down here now and I'd like to enjoy a little of it. You could send it express and insure it if necessary. I could bring it with me Christmas. If you can send it I'll be awfully glad and I'll take good care of it. Write when you can.

Love,
Orlie

Orlie Meskimen

▼

Camp Claiborne, LA

November 15, 1941

Dear Folks,

Everything is pretty much the same here. The weather is real warm now. The temperature ranges around 65 or 70 all the time. I suppose it's rather chilly up there by this time isn't it?

I wonder if you could send me the shotgun when the pheasant season is over. The duck hunting is the best down here of any place in the nation and I'd like to get in on it. I've gone a couple of times but since I had no gun it wasn't much fun. I'd bring it home at Christmas time.

I hear from LaVonne Butler real often. I got a letter from her today also the picture I'm sending you. It isn't a bad picture although the sun rather glared on her glasses. Please send it back after you've posted judgment on her. I haven't heard from Diane. But then it doesn't matter so maybe it's just as well. She evidently is through with me this time.

I'll send the album soon. I nearly have it finished now. Maybe I'll have to wait until the first of the month so I'll have the money to send it.

Tell Clare "hello" and I'll write him soon.

Love,
Orlie

Dear Folks, Love Orlie

▼

Camp Claiborne, LA

November 19, 1941

Dear Folks,

Well how are you by this time? I am fine. I received your card today and was glad to hear from you. Don't worry about the boxes – I haven't received them yet but I'll get them if they're addressed correctly. I'll be glad to get them. Thanks a million.

Tomorrow is Thanksgiving Day for the fellows in the service here in the Army. Each man will get 1-1/4 pounds of turkey and all the extras required to fill out the meal. We only get the one day off so Friday we go back to work.

About the tale Diane is telling around. It's not true as far as I know anything about it. Probably she just wants to start something. I wrote her a letter and gave her the devil about it. I told her to keep her nose out of my business since what I do now doesn't concern her anymore. LaVonne Butler is a swell kid and regardless of what Diane says she will still be OK for my money. Diane seems like a dream to me now. I told her that and also that if I never saw her again it would be too soon.

It's raining a soft gentle rain here tonight. It's rather warm. I'm writing in my shorts with the tent rolled up so you can see it's rather warm.

Well, I'll close for this time. I'm so busy it's hard to find time to write.

Love, Orlie
P.S. Send the gun if possible.

Orlie Meskimen

▼

Camp Claiborne, LA

November 24, 1941

Dear Folks,

Just a line to let you know I received the box and was very glad to get it. The candy was delicious. The weather is rather nasty here today. It's been raining since yesterday and it's rather cool. I am in charge of quarters today. This means I am on duty from 6:00 til 10:00 in the evening. It makes rather a long day. How is everything in Shellsburg now? I got a letter from Clare today, also Bob Bergen and a card from either Claude Blattler or John Irish. Have Dad find out which one it was, will you?

Love,
Orlie

Dear Folks, Love Orlie

Camp Claiborne, LA

November 24, 1941

Dear Folks,

This letter will be rather short because I haven't much time but I'll write as long as I can.

I wonder if you would send my diamond ring down. I've found a pretty good place to sell it and I'll need the money for my Christmas furlough. Also please send the gun. I can lock it in my foot locker and it will be perfectly safe. You could wrap it in rags and then a gunny sack.

The weather is much better now. It's stopped raining and turned a little chilly. But we're still wearing cottons.

I'm glad you like LaVonne's looks. She's really a nice kid. So clean and straight from the shoulder. She writes to me nearly every day. Well, I guess I'd better close.

Love,
Orlie

Orlie Meskimen

▼

Camp Claiborne, LA

December 1, 1941

Dear Folks,

    Sunday night – so I'll write you a few lines. That was Claude who sent me the card. I got a letter from him yesterday. I wrote Erdie and thanked her for the candy. It was very good – the cakes were extra good. I'll probably be home soon but the fellow I spoke about won't be with me I guess. He isn't going anywhere for Christmas. You needn't bother to send the gun. There's so little time left. Yes, I've got ducks several times.

Love,
Orlie

Dear Folks, Love Orlie

▼

Camp Claiborne, LA

December 3, 1941

Dear Folks,

Well, how are you by this time? I am fine, but have been pretty busy since I've been back. I've been going to non-commissioned officer's school every day. We've been studying 50 caliber machine guns, 37 M.M. anti-tank guns, grenades, scouting and patrolling, motorized and mechanized marches. All of this is very interesting and will help me no end in the future. As yet no further promotions have been made but the big break promises to come soon.

Beyond a doubt I will be home sometime this month. Just when my furlough will come is kind of hard to say just now, but I'm assured of getting one soon. Tom, Spurgeon, King and myself will probably all be home at the same time. There's a big possibility I will be home before the 15th of the month. My furlough calls for sixteen days this time – one more day than the last.

I'm going to have two teeth pulled sometime this week. They've finally started to fix our teeth. All extractions come first and then the fillings and cleaning. My teeth were placed in 1st class so evidently they aren't so bad. The captain who examined them said I had two to be extracted and six to be filled. I hope they do a good job. They just put in all the latest equipment so maybe they will.

We are all to receive Wassermann blood tests soon again. As you probably know the Wassermann is the only positive check for syphilis. They had a big epidemic of crabs here this last week and we were all examined each day. Of course, don't tell anyone about it because we wouldn't want it spread around. I was fortunate enough never to get them. Maybe I'd better knock on wood.

Well, I guess I'd better close for this time. I'll try to write a better letter next time.

Love,
Orlie

Dear Folks, Love Orlie

> Dec. 8, 1941 – Arrived in New Orleans for guard duty.
>
> Pearl Harbor was the scene of a devastating surprise attack by Japanese forces on December 7, 1941. Just before 8 a.m. on that Sunday morning, hundreds of Japanese fighter planes descended on the base, where they managed to destroy or damage nearly 20 American naval vessels and over 300 airplanes. More than 2,400 Americans died in the attack, including civilians, and another 1,000 people were wounded. The day after the assault, President Franklin D. Roosevelt asked Congress to declare war on Japan.

―――――▼―――――

New Orleans, LA

December 11, 1941

Dear Folks,

    I received your letter today and was glad to hear from you. As you have probably noticed, I've been moved. We moved last Sunday and have been so busy since I just now got time to write. We are just 15 miles out of New Orleans on the Gulf side. How long we will be here or where we will go is hard to say. But don't worry about us – we'll be OK. See Tom's mother as often as you can. She will probably worry a lot. As far as us seeing action, well, we won't be afraid and are anxious right now to try a little of it.

    That was surely too bad about Harold Hite. Tom got a letter from his mother yesterday and she told him about it.

Orlie Meskimen

Eileen must feel pretty bad about it all.

We heard over the radio that we are now actually at war with Germany, Italy and Japan. Now that we are at war with all them, Russia will understandably give us air bases from which our bombers can raid various Japanese cities and other objectives. This war, in my estimation, will be all over inside of one year.

I won't be home for Christmas. All furloughs have been canceled. Perhaps a little later on I will be able to though. Well, I guess I'd better close for this time.

Love,
Orlie
P.S. Write and take care of yourselves. I will send the gun home as soon as it gets here.

Dear Folks, Love Orlie

Dec. 23, 1941 – Returned to Camp Claiborne

▼

Camp Claiborne, LA

December 27, 1941

Dear Folks,

Well, I got back okay and am now busy getting settled. I found John around ten o'clock so we went out together for the rest of the night. Everything is pretty much the same here. The weather is very nice. So warm and sunny. My address is the same as before we went to New Orleans. I surely had a lot of mail down here. I've been pretty busy reading it all. Well, I guess I'd better close for this time. I'll write a letter later.

Love, Orlie

▼

Camp Claiborne, LA

December 31, 1941

Dear Folks,

We're moving out this morning. I don't know where we're going but I'll tell you as soon as I know. You can write me at this address if you like and I'll probably get it. I'll write again soon. I guess they called Tom back from his furlough. Too bad he couldn't have finished his time. Did he come to visit you while he was home? Write.

Love, Orlie

Orlie Meskimen

Jan. 1, 1942 – The 133rd moved to Fort Dix, New Jersey to prepare for embarkation

▼

Train to Camp Dix, New Jersey

January 1, 1942

Dear Folks,

    I am writing this letter on the train so it's apt to be a little scrawly. We are going to Camp Dix, New Jersey. How long we will be there or where we will go is hard to say. Don't worry about me – I'll be okay. Maybe I'll get a chance to see Bernice and Dorothy while I'm there. I've lost Bernice's address. Will you send it to me as soon as possible. Use my old address until I forward you the new one. Write me often. Mail will be slow from now on out.

Love, Orlie

Dear Folks, Love Orlie

▼

Indianapolis, IN

January 2, 1942

Dear Folks,

Well, we're well on our way now so I'll drop you another card. Hope you are fine or as well as I am. The weather here is quite a change as compared with Louisiana. I suppose the weather there is cold now too. I'll write you a letter from our ultimate destination when we get there. Write me often and tell everyone else to write. I'll enjoy all the letters I can get now. Tell Jack and Dan to write me when I send you my new address.

Love, Orlie

▼

Trenton, NJ

January 3, 1942

Dear Folks,

We arrived at Camp Dix okay and are fairly well settled. You can write me here. My address is the same except that it's Camp Dix, New Jersey, instead of Camp Claiborne. I don't know how long we will be here but it probably won't be long. Send me Dorothy and Bernice's address right away. Maybe I'll get to see them. I'll write as often as I can and you do the same.

Love, Orlie

Orlie Meskimen

▼

Camp Dix, New Jersey

January 4, 1942

Dear Folks,

We arrived here yesterday and are getting fairly well settled. It's snowing and raining here today and so, of course, it's rather miserable. But I expect the future will bring days that will be much more miserable. You may rest assured that we're going to sail within the next ten days for some island. So this address will be only temporary but if you write me via air mail as soon as you receive this. Send me a couple of books of stamps along too if possible. We can't get out to buy them as they have us quarantined until we embark to a sailing point. Probably we will fight Japs and you can be sure they will be a sorry bunch of guys when we finish with them.

How are things at home? I suppose the weather is bad there too. I hope we go to one of the tropical islands where it's warm. I'm getting tired of this wet, cold weather.

Tell everyone "hello" and tell them not to write until I get a permanent address. Of course, you folks write often – the letters will reach me sometime. LaVonne B. wrote me three letters that I got before we left. It's hard to tell how many more I have behind me. My address will be rather shaky from now on. Don't worry about me – I'll be okay. I'll never tell you when I do go into action so that will lessen your worries. We're all set here and straining at the leash.

Write Russell's & Bernice and thank them for the cookies and the cigarette case. Russell's sent the cookies.

Dear Folks, Love Orlie

Tell them I can't get writing equipment. Send me all of Sam's kid's addresses so I can write to them. Tell everyone to write me and I'll try to answer their letters as best I can.

Well, guess I'd better close for this time. I'll write a card when I can. Send me a few cards when you can. Naturally our payroll hasn't reached us yet but as soon as it does I'll send Shipley's money. It should come within the next week.

Love,
Orlie

Orlie Meskimen

January 7, 1942

Dear Folks,

Just a line to let you know I'm okay and hoping you are the same. I've a new address which is on the front. Write me as soon as you get this and I'll probably get it soon. As yet I've received no mail since I left Claiborne. But for that matter no one has. Our mail hasn't caught up with us yet. You will have to excuse this card – I've been carrying it around with me for some time. Write when you can and I'll write you the same way.

Love,
Orlie

Dear Folks, Love Orlie

▼

Hq. Det, New York, NY

January 8, 1942

Dear Folks,

Well, I'm still OK. The weather here is fine. But rather chilly. We're having all our teeth fixed up and they are going to x-ray us tonight to be sure we are all physically fit.

I signed out an allotment this morning. The government will send you $25 each month to save for me. It will start March 1st. We are going to be paid Saturday and I'll send the $15 for Shipley then. Thank him for me. This allotment will save $300 a year for me. When my ten dollar raise comes through I'll send $10 per month cash extra home. I want you to save it to get dad a set of false teeth. You take the first $25 grandma and whatever it takes to pay you back from the second. I guess I owe you around $35.

We don't know just for sure when we'll leave here but it can't be very long. I'll drop you a line just before we leave. After we push off it may be from two weeks to a month before you hear from me because naturally I won't be able to mail any letters from the boat.

We expect a little mail to trickle through tomorrow. I'll surely be glad to get mine. It gets rather lonesome when the letters are cut off. I suppose we will have mail deliveries once a month or once every two weeks. However, write to me just as you would in Camp Claiborne. I got a telegram from LaVonne Butler last night. It was a night letter. She's pretty worried about me and the future. She said she was going to send me a ring of her mother's to carry with me.

I told her to keep it then if I didn't come back it wouldn't be lost.

If you can send me the stamps and post cards I asked for some time ago please do so. It's really impossible to get them here. I'm nearly out of everything in the writing material line. I still have a couple of cards and several stamps.

I took out $2,000 worth more insurance in your name. Have you received the policy yet? Please let me know so I'll be sure of it. I don't want to be paying for something I'm not getting. That makes $3,000 I have now. Well, I guess I'd better close. Tell everyone "hello".

Love,
Orlie
Write

Dear Folks, Love Orlie

▼

Hq. Det, New York, NY

January 11, 1942

Dear Folks,

    Just a few lines to let you know I received your latest letters. I got four letters from you today also the cards and stamps. Possibly soon now my letters will cease for some time, possibly two weeks or a month. But don't worry – I'll be okay. LaVonne Butler's address is 1320 30th Street Northwest. Write her occasionally. She's very good to write me. Tell everyone hello and tell them to write to me. I got a letter from Dorothy today. Maybe I'll get to see her.

Orlie

Orlie Meskimen

▼

Camp Dix, NJ

January 13, 1942

Dear Folks,

Well, today is Tuesday and its been a rather nice day here. I suppose the weather is still pretty nasty there. I read in the Gazette about the big snowstorm and cold you have had there.

This will probably be my last letter to you due to circumstances beyond my control. Circumstances which I have already explained and I'm sure you understand. However, you continue to write as always and the letters will reach me. My address will be the same as on the outside of this envelope. Don't worry about us.

LaVonne B. has been very good to write me. I get letters from her nearly every day. She has been much better than Diane ever was. She is going to have a big picture made for me. Also she is getting a rosary for me and having it blessed. She's a swell kid. She says two rosaries for me every night. Also she's wired me once since I got here. Diane has written me too but her letters don't count any more. It's true LaVonne B. wanted to get married but I couldn't see my way clear.

I don't remember whether I told you before or not but Tom is back with us. He has been here several days. Homer

Dear Folks, Love Orlie

Woodson also is transferred over here now. So we're pretty much all together now.

    Well, this is short but I can't think of much to write.

Love, Orlie
P.S. Write when you can.

Orlie Meskimen

On Jan. 15, 1942, Headquarters with Regl. Hdqrs. Co., 1st Bn., Anti-Tank Co., plus Service Co. sailed from New York for overseas duty. These troops were the first American soldiers to set foot on European soil in World War II as they arrived in Belfast, North Ireland. The remainder of the Regiment left the States on Feb. 19, 1942 and arrived in the British Isles on March 2nd.

Departure Date	Embarkation Place	Vessel	Units on Board	Debarkation Place	Arrival Date
01-15-42	New York, NY	*HMTS Strathaird*	34th Infantry Division (Advance Command Post of Headquarters Company; 133rd Infantry Regiment less 2nd and 3nd Battalions, 151st Field Artillery Battalion)	with *USAT Chateau Thierry* Belfast, Northern Ireland	01-26-42
01-15-42	New York, NY	*USAT Chateau Thierry*	34th Infantry Division (det of 109th Medical Battalion [136th Medical Regiment], det of 109th Quartermaster Battalion, Company "A" of 109th Engineer Combat Battalion, det of Military Police Platoon); det of 112th Engineer Combat Battalion; 10th Station Hospital; det of 63rd Signal Battalion	with *HMTS Strathaird* Belfast, Northern Ireland	01-26-42

JANUARY 1942
NORTHERN IRELAND

Location unknown

January 27, 1942

Dear Folks,

Just a few lines to let you know I'm okay. We got here yesterday and are getting fairly well settled now. Whether you already know it or not, we're in [redacted]. Of course, I can't tell you just where. The voyage took us [redacted] days. All in all it wasn't such a bad trip. I was never seasick but my stomach was slightly uneasy for a couple of days. I guess that's about all there is to say about the trip.

The weather is rather damp and rainy here. But it isn't very cold and everything is a little green. I believe it's about the most beautiful country I've ever seen. It's a little like Iowa except for the terrain. The land is very rough and hilly – almost mountainous. The people have very little brogue. All in all, they treat us very nice. Accommodations are much better than we expected.

How is the weather in Iowa by this time? I suppose

Orlie Meskimen

it's rather cold and snowy by this time. It was pretty cold when we left New Jersey. It was too bad I didn't get to see Bernice or Dorothy. Pogles invited me up for a weekend but naturally I didn't get to go. It would have been nice if I could have gone.

Have you written to LaVonne Butler yet? If you haven't already done so yet, please do it soon. She's an awfully nice kid. She's done a lot for me – far more than Diane ever did. If you can have her up for a Sunday or some other day I'm sure you will like her. She hated it because she didn't get to meet you while I was home the other time.

We are all together yet. Tom, John and myself. In fact, the outfit never will be broken up. King, of course, is with us too. Have they drafted any more Shellsburg fellows? I suppose they will be getting more of them now.

My letters may not come as often now as they did before. Of course, you are able to understand why this will be. I'll write as often as convenient and I want you to write as often as you like.

Sincerely with love,
Orlie

Dear Folks, Love Orlie

▼

Location unknown

January 28, 1942

Dear Folks,

I've already written one letter just yesterday but since I've a request to make I thought I'd write again. You see, it's almost impossible to buy cigarettes and razor blades here so I wondered if you could send me some as soon as possible. If you could send me two cartons of Camel cigarettes and several packages of blades each month it would surely help. You could use money from the monthly allotment sent each month. It's possible to buy them here but they're so terribly expensive it's hard for us to afford them. I am going to have LaVonne send me an additional 2 cartons each month because I require about four of them per month.

If you see any of the following people give them my address and tell them to write me: Bob, Edna Husted, Jack & Dan, Oscar's kids, etc. I'll be glad to hear from all of them. Tell Bernice, Dorothy and Russell's to write me too. They were very good to send me Christmas gifts.

Naturally our letters are censored so you can understand why I don't tell you anything about what we're doing. Of course it's not difficult to understand why this censorship is absolutely necessary. But don't worry about us – we'll be alright.

Be sure to give Shipley the money from the first allotment. He was very good to advance the money. Thank him for it. It surely came in handy.

Don't try to send me any other boxes other than the

cigarettes and blades. Otherwise you will probably have to pay a customs tax. An occasional package of gum wouldn't hurt either.

I guess I'd better close for this time. It's almost time to go to bed. I'll write more later on.

Love, Orlie

P.S. We have a fellow by the name of Olson from Newhall with us now. I enjoy talking to him because we've a lot of mutual friends.

Dear Folks, Love Orlie

▼

Northern Ireland

February 2, 1942

Dear Folks,

I'll write you a few more lines today. I suppose you are rather anxious to hear from me since I'm across the Atlantic. We still haven't received any mail from over there but expect some soon. We will all be glad to hear from you folks at home. It seems like years since we've had mail.

Since we've been here we have had to exchange our money for British. It was rather hard to understand at first but we're rapidly catching on now. Their denominations are half pence, pence, three pence, six pence, shillings, two shillings, half crowns, half pounds, pounds, etc.

I can tell you for sure now that we're in Northern Ireland. Don't confuse this with the Irish Free State – it's south of here. Also I can tell you I have visited Belfast. The weather is rainy but warm and everything is fairly green. That's about all I can tell you about this country. Of course, you can understand this. We have electric lights and small coal stoves.

I am going to mail this letter via Trans-Atlantic clipper. It's quite possible this letter will reach you before the two I have written before. Don't let the postage on it confuse you. One of these stamps costs one pence over here. In American currency it would cost approximately two cents. I thought I would send one this way just for fun.

I have been to town several times. Of course I can't tell you what town it is. Everything is much different than back there. There are a few American cars over here – mostly Chevrolet's. Their cars are a lot different than ours. Steering wheels on the right side and they drive down the left side of the road.

If you see Marvin Holmes tell him to write to Tom and I. We don't have much time to write to everyone. Also any of the other fellows we were friendly with. I suppose Marvin will have to come into the Army any day now. Has Don G. received his draft papers yet? Or is he old enough?

Have you seen Clare lately? Tell him to write to me too. I'll drop him a line one of these days. I've got to write to LaVonne Butler tonight yet too. We haven't received any mail yet but should get some soon. We're getting rather anxious for mail.

Today is February 5. So you see its been several days since I started this letter. I won't be able to send this via air mail. Regulations have been changed and we can't send them that way anymore. I'll get this ready to mail now.

Love,
Orlie
P.S. We've making cocoa over our stove tonight. Sure tastes good!

Dear Folks, Love Orlie

Northern Ireland

February 20, 1942

Dear Folks,

Well, I'll write you a few lines tonight. We've had no mail from you folks at home but maybe we'll get some soon. It's rather hard to write when it's been so long since last I heard from you. Then too the censorship naturally limits the things we can say.

Did you receive a card stating that I had reached my destination? If you did, did you tell LaVonne Butler? I know she worries and I'd like to have her feel that I was OK. Write to her occasionally and invite her up for a visit now and then too. She's an awfully nice kid and I like her very much. She's so much better than Diane.

What sort of work are you doing these days dad? I suppose the work situation is rather slack as usual this time of year. The farm work should begin soon though. But I guess there isn't much doing even on the farms until the later part of May. Did you cut any wood this winter? I suppose Merl Wayson wanted some cut. I sort of wish I could go cut some right now.

We had American cigarettes and beer issued to us recently. You can send the cigarettes along anyway. You can never tell when the supply will be cut and we won't be able to get any. I'll always be able to use them at any rate.

Tell Earl and Dick to write me, and I'll try to write them when I find time and can think of anything to say.

Orlie Meskimen

I think a lot of them and all the rest. I'd like to hear from Louise and Elmer too. Also Jack and Don.

We all have colds and can't seem to get rid of them. They're not very severe colds but just hard to shake off.

February 25, 1942: It's been several days since I started this letter but I've been rather busy and just haven't gotten around to write.

I have been going out occasionally with a girl named Annette Gallagher. Nothing serious at all but she is nice and it's a pleasure to be with her. There isn't much to do except see a movie or go dancing. The dance bands over here aren't so hot so we don't dance much.

Well, I guess I'd better close for this time. I hope to hear from you soon.

Love, Orlie

Dear Folks, Love Orlie

▼

Northern Ireland

March 3, 1942

Dear Folks,

Today we finally got mail! I received seven letters from you and Clare. I guess there is still mail that hasn't been distributed. It surely seemed good to get mail from the states. I also received letters from LaVonne Butler, Diane, and Marlene Koopman. In all I got sixteen letters so far. Diane would kind of like to hear from me. Personally, she hasn't much chance – unless she does a lot of explaining.

The picture you sent was of me. Along with me, reading from left to right are: myself, John Emery, Kelley, Starkey, and Joe Nemec. You should have pictures of all of them except Starkey there at home. Starkey is a new man – transferred from another outfit when we went up to war strength. As far as how we are doing over here goes, well, I just can't say much. If mail doesn't seem to come quite as often as it should, don't worry. Mail is slow to leave here and then, or course, the mail boats must thread their way through the Atlantic just as we did when we came across. But I'll write once a week or so. Watch the papers because we quite frequently have our pictures taken.

The day before yesterday was pay day. You should have received the two allotments by now. Also I sent three pounds via cable. This in American money amounts to $12.06. It's compulsory that we sent it in pounds – of course, it is exchanged for American money before it gets to you. I want this to go on dad's teeth. I'll send some each month and I want no excuses for not getting the teeth. You can save it until you get enough to pay for them or pay as I send it. Probably it would be better to wait though because maybe I couldn't send it some months. Don't skimp – get good ones!

Tell Clare "hello" and I'll try to write to him one of these days. So he couldn't get in the Army. Well, it's just as good. Army life would have been a pretty rigid affair for him. Maybe he can find some work in Cedar Rapids now.

I was rather sorry to hear about Rhoda Ann Weichanan. It's a shame Blattlers have to do the way they are. It would have been much better for them to have been married. For Dick it will soon be forgotten but for Rhoda Ann it will always be a black mark. I don't think it's Claude as much as it is Violet. I changed ink as you probably noticed. Also I was sorry to hear about Willard McCorkle – I guess he always was rather nervous.

Tom, John, King, Homer and myself are all here together. Homer was transferred into our battalion so he's here with us too. Well, I guess I'd better close for this time. It's so hard to write. Maybe when the mail starts coming regularly it will be easier.

And, dad, if we have to give them hell as you say – we're just the boys who can do it.

Love,
Orlie
P.S. Write.

Dear Folks, Love Orlie

▼

Northern Ireland

March 14, 1942

Dear Folks,

Well, today is Saturday and since we have the afternoon off I'll drop you a few lines. It has been raining here today and is pretty miserable. But it shouldn't be long until spring now.

I guess I told you about my being sick. I had laryngitis and pharyngitis acute. I lost my voice almost a week and one half ago and haven't entirely regained it yet. I was marked "quarters" from February 28 until March 8th. This means the medics ordered me to stay in my quarters for that period of time. My throat was never really sore and I didn't feel so bad. Lots of the fellows have colds but nothing serious.

I got two more letters yesterday – one from you and one from LaVonne. They had been mislaid somewhere. Probably they were sent to another unit. They were both old letters – postmarked sometime in January. But still nice to get.

Well, my two dollar raise is through now. It came of course February 10. So I 'm making $64 per month. There are rumors of another 20% raise for foreign service. I surely hope it goes through.

I have been out in the open country a lot lately. The farmers surely manage things in a funny way. Their fences are mounds of earth about three feet wide and three feet high with hedges on them. Every available inch of soil is utilized. All the fields are irregular in shape. It's only rarely you can find one that's any where near squared. All small grains are called corn. And, as far as corn goes, they just don't raise it because of the shallowness of the surface soil. They are getting ready to plant potatoes now.

Tom, John and George are all well and send their regards. It's nice that we are all together yet. I was afraid for awhile that Tom wouldn't catch up with us.

Well, I guess I'll have to close for this time. Write me when you can.

Love,
Orlie
P.S. Here are some picture cards I decided to enclose. I just got back from town.

Dear Folks, Love Orlie

▼

Northern Ireland

March 21, 1942

Dear Folks,

Today is the first day of spring and it's been a lovely day over here. Tonight is pretty swell too – so clear and bright. I guess it's about time for spring though!

I just got back from town a few minutes ago. I went in right after dinner and it's now ten o'clock. I didn't do much but just loaf around and see a movie. There really isn't much more to do. I'll surely be glad to see old Cedar Rapids again where there is something to do. I plan to sleep late tomorrow and sort of catch up on my sleep. It seems I can't get enough sleep anymore.

Say, one of these days I want you to mail LaVonne Butler $10 from my allotment money. I bought her a robe on credit but it was never sent to me or else it got lost somewhere. She can use the money for anything she likes and I really want her to have it. She's been awfully good to me.

I used a typewriter to address this envelope. It's been so long since last I used one that I had a tough time of it. It belongs to one of the fellows in my hut but I can use it anytime I like.

We haven't received any more mail since the other batch but maybe I'll be able to write a few letters before we do. It's hard to write much when the news isn't coming in very regularly.

Well, I guess I'd better close for this time. I'll try to send a little extra money home again this month. If you want to,

Orlie Meskimen

dad, you can use the money whenever there's enough there to pay for the teeth. Early this summer would probably be a good time to get it over with. Bye.

Love,
Orlie
P.S. Here's another card for you grandma.

Dear Folks, Love Orlie

Northern Ireland

March 29, 1942

Dear Folks,

Just a few lines to let you know I am fine and in good spirits. We got a little mail Thursday but I only got one letter. It was from Uncle Fred. I suppose we'll get more soon. He said Ethyl Meskimen was in Washington working for some firm out there. She called him long distance and I guess he was pretty surprised.

The weather has been pretty good lately. I suppose its nice over there too. One can readily understand why they call Ireland the "Emerald Isle" – it's because everything is so green all the year 'round.

I just got back from town a while ago. The blackouts are pretty hard to get used to. It's so awfully dark. We have them every night over here. It's especially hard when you come out of a brightly lighted place. You bump into people and people bump into you. Lots of the fellows have fun picking up blackout dates. You really can't tell what you're getting until you get into a lighted place.

By the way, I guess we're getting a 20% raise for foreign pay. This will raise my pay so I am going to try to raise my allotment to $50 per month. I won't be able to send any extra this month but I will next month. Be sure and get the teeth dad. I should be able to save a little nest egg by the time I get home again. My monthly pay will be $74.80 now which really isn't so bad. It's more than a staff sergeant in the states gets. He draws $72.

Orlie Meskimen

Tom is asleep just now but he always sends his regards. We wrote to Marvin and Guy Boyer yesterday. I suppose Brink will soon be in the Army now. I suppose you have had to register, haven't you dad? Fred said they were registering up to 65. He also said one of Will Hall's boys was over here. He's going to send me his address and I'll look him up.

Well, I guess I'd better close for this time. I know my letters are short but I just can't seem to think of anything to write.

All my love,
Orlie
P.S. Here's a couple of stamps Fred sent me. They're no good over here.

Dear Folks, Love Orlie

▼

Northern Ireland

April 5, 1942

Dear Folks,

Just a few lines to tell you we got a little more mail. I got letters from you and LaVonne and Diane. I was glad to hear you had finally heard from me. We only got a few letters this time but maybe we'll get more soon. It's coming in awfully slow.

I'm so glad LaVonne was up to visit you folks. She also wrote me about it and she said she liked all you folks and had a nice time. I guess she thought "Jeep" was okay. She's an awfully nice kid – I sincerely hope you like her. She was wondering if she should smoke in front of you or not but I told her I thought you wouldn't mind. It's really nothing – most girls do. Far more girls smoke over here than in the States. Have her come as often as she likes. She says it brings me closer when she sees you folks.

The weather over here has been a little rainy but, all in all, it isn't so bad. It's pretty warm and the sun does occasionally break through. It's windy here today – like a day in March back there.

I sent you some Easter flowers the other day, mother. I hope you liked them. I also hope you got them today. Most of the fellows sent flowers to either their mothers or girls. I should have sent LaVonne something but I just couldn't afford it.

Well, I guess I'll have to close for this time. I'll try to write a little each week. Happy Easter to all of you. I know

Orlie Meskimen

this won't reach you for some time. My thoughts are with all of you today anyway.

Love,
Orlie
P.S. Tell Clare "hello" and tell him to keep writing.

Dear Folks, Love Orlie

Northern Ireland

April 21, 1942

Dear Folks,

Well, how are you by this time? I am still fine. I got three more letters from you today and two from LaVonne. Two of them were postmarked in March and one in February. Both of LaVonne's were in March. Also I got the gum, blades and cigarettes. Thanks.

Did you know I got a letter a week or so ago from Anna Fee? She sent me two addresses of relatives we have here. Very probably I will never get to visit them because both of them are quite some distance away and transportation facilities are not so good.

I'm glad you like LaVonne and hope she continues to visit you folks. I think a great deal of her. I knew she would be rather shy about meeting you but would be right at home after she became acquainted. I know she will enjoy being there with you. She had lots of fun and was looking forward to the time she could call on you again. Her mother does look a lot like you, mom.

We are going to start writing via air mail. This will speed it up considerably. Of course, I won't write all of them that way, but will write a few that way. LaVonne writes by air mail and her letters seem to reach me sooner than yours. Let her read my letters if you like. There's usually nothing in them that really matters anyway.

About the cigarettes, you can cut the amount down to one carton a month if you like – we're getting quite a few of them lately. I'll always need the razor blades and gum though.

    Well, I guess I'll close. Always let Clare read my letters, they're for all of you.

All of my love,
Orlie

Dear Folks, Love Orlie

▼

Northern Ireland

May 11, 1942

Dear Folks,

Well, we received mail again today and I got letters from you, LaVonne, Diane, Maxson's, Edna Husted and Orville Graham. So I've a considerable amount of writing to do. I have such a terrible time trying to write a few letters. And I also got a letter from Earl Mason. I'll answer it tonight too.

I'm glad you like the roses. I sent some more flowers of some kind for Mother's Day. I ordered a plant. I hope it grows for you.

I'm glad you're getting your teeth fixed, dad. They will be troublesome for awhile but in time you will be much better off. I had two pulled and four filled last week. My teeth are all good now. I'm glad you got your glasses too, mother. We from Shellsburg that are over here are all in good health. I don't see Homer very often but the rest of us are all together.

I laughed till I was sick about grandma's teeth. It must have been really funny.

It was surely too bad about Tiny Sanders wife dying. She hadn't been sick, had she? I always thought there was something the matter with Willard McCorkle so that really wasn't much of a surprise.

Did you know Bob Bergen and Edna Husted were engaged? They were engaged at Christmas time but didn't tell anyone then.

Orlie Meskimen

Well, I guess I'll have to close for this time. It's so hard to think of anything to say. You know, I think of all of you often.

Love,
Orlie

Dear Folks, Love Orlie

▼

Northern Ireland

May 21, 1942

Dear Folks,

This will be just a few short lines to let you know I'm okay and to send you these pictures. They aren't so good but they're new ones at least. There was too much sunlight the day we took them. But maybe they will give you a vague idea of what Ireland is like.

I was glad to hear about Bob. I really think he made a good deal. Edna is a grand kid and, of course you know what I think about Bob. He deserves so much more than Marian would ever have given him.

We lost our 1st Sergeant today. He was transferred into another outfit. I surely hated to see him go. He was about the best fellow I ever met. But maybe it was all for the best.

I am getting some more pictures soon and will send you some of them if they pass the censor. And maybe you can send me some too.

Well, dad, how's the store teeth treating you? I imagine they will seem strange for awhile but you'll get used to them before long.

I hope you like these pictures. I'm getting mail from you regularly now. Tell everyone "hello" for me. Especially the Davis's and the little boys.

Love,
Orlie
P.S. Use this new address.

Orlie Meskimen

May 28, 1942 – The Regiment assembled in the vicinity of Caledon, Northern Ireland for intensive training and maneuvers

▼

Northern Ireland

June 3, 1942

Dear Folks,

Here I go again – I received two letters from you yesterday. I was surely glad to hear from you. Also I heard from LaVonne Butler. She told me all about the robe and the hose. She's a grand kid and deserves the best of everything.

I was rather sorry to hear about Diane being sick. I never received your original letter telling me about it. What sort of hemorrhage was it?

All of us are fine. We have everything we need and are well satisfied. Tom has a driving job now and seems to enjoy it. We are all caught up on the films over here so we get considerable diversion from the movies. When we first came over most of the shows were old and we had seen quite a lot of them. I saw a very good one last night entitled, "So Ends Our Night."

I haven't seen either Vogt or Spurgeon yet but I saw Woodson and he said he saw Vogt.

I am going to send more pictures the next time I write. I am sending this air mail so the extra weight would make it too heavy.

Dear Folks, Love Orlie

Well, I guess I'll have to close for this time. Tell everyone "hello" for me.

Love, Orlie
P.S. Use this new address.

Orlie Meskimen

▼

Northern Ireland

June 24, 1942

Dear Folks,

I received several more letters from you a day or so ago. Also the second batch of cigarettes. Send them at least once a month because we may have difficulty getting them over here. You won't need to send any more razor blades until I tell you to send more.

I got quite a little mail in this last batch. I received letters from you, Uncle Fred, Jo Popenhagen, LaVonne, Diane, and also Junior Reynolds. Junior is a nice kid – he wrote me a very good letter. He said he was coming to visit you folks some day.

The weather over here has been pretty good lately. I suppose it's really nice over there by this time. Some of the fellows have been fishing over here. In fact, two fellows caught two pike about 20 inches long last night. I guess there are some pretty good salmon in some of the mountain streams.

Some of us listen to the Command Performance program. I usually listen if I'm here. We don't get America very often unless the program is sent directly to us. However, some of the British programs are pretty good.

Well, I guess this will be all for this time. I'm sending the Stars and Stripes too.

Love,
Orlie

Dear Folks, Love Orlie

▼

Northern Ireland

June 27, 1942

Dear Folks,

    Received several letters from you just recently. So glad to hear from you. Also very glad to get the pictures. I'll send a few in this letter. Hope you like them.

    I haven't been able to secure air mail stamps or my letters would reach you much sooner. If you'd like to hear from me a little more regularly send me a few air mail stamps. The service runs between 8 and 15 days. We have "V" mail now and I'll write my next letter to you on it. Probably you've heard of it. Our letters are photographed and the film sent to the states. There it is developed, the negatives printed and sent to you.

    We are all well and in the best of spirits so don't worry about us. Tom sleeps near me and I see George pretty often.

    John got his walking papers from May! I never thought it would ever happen. But I guess I know from experience that it can.

    I suppose your mouth is healing up, dad. Hope you will soon have your teeth and have no trouble with them.

    Well, folks, guess I'd better close. Good luck and all my love.

Orlie
P.S. Got a nice letter from Louise Waller.

Orlie Meskimen

▼

Northern Ireland

July 11, 1942

Dear Folks,

    I am sorry I haven't written during the past few days but I haven't been here. I'll try to write a few lines today though and another letter soon.

    We are all well and happy. I see Homer real often these days. He seems to be getting much heavier. Mail comes through to us pretty regularly, although I didn't get any the last two deliveries. They were air mail though.

    I am sending the latest issue of the Stars and Stripes. Hope you enjoy them and keep them for me. It was edited during the other war and has been started again this time.

    I suppose you folks spent a nice 4th of July. We were busy so it seemed just like any other day to me. The weather is pretty cool here and so it doesn't seem like it was July. It hardly seems possible that fall and winter will soon be here again. I guess winter over here isn't very severe though.

    I was glad to hear Arlene Peterman is doing so well. She's surely had her share of hard times. But even at her age an education will still be a good deal.

    Well, folks, guess I'll have to close for this time. Write when you can.

Love,
Orlie

Dear Folks, Love Orlie

▼

Northern Ireland

July 12, 1942

Dear Folks,

I will write you a few lines on this new type of mail now being offered to the services. Hope you are able to read my erratic writing. I will do my very best though.

I got a nice letter from LaVonne yesterday but none from you. However it was air mail though and you never write that way. She plans to visit soon again.

What did you folks do over the 4th of July? I was on duty so naturally mine wasn't as pleasant as usual. I suppose it was pretty hot there and probably rained before the day was over.

Well, folks, I know this is rather short but, as you can see, the paper is limited. Hope you are all well and happy. How's the teeth coming dad? Take care of yourselves. Write!!

Love,
Orlie

Orlie Meskimen

▼

Northern Ireland

July 25, 1942

Dear Folks,

Received two letters from you today and you said you hadn't heard from me since June 3rd. The reason for that is because we have trouble getting air mail stamps. I managed to get three today but ordinarily I can't get them. If you will take some of my allotment money and send me some you will get letters more often. Air mail is pretty fast. The letters I got from you today were dated July 11 and July 14, and that's pretty good.

I got a carton of cigarettes from Rube Senft the other day but never seem to get many from you. Be sure you send them at least once a month. Also the stamps and gum.

I was rather sorry to hear about Schotterback. I guess there must have been something wrong with him. There always is when a person does that.

How are the store teeth coming by this time? I suppose you're getting used to them. You should feel better. I've had two back teeth pulled since I've been over here and I believe I feel better.

I've gained some weight here lately and feel pretty good. My teeth are all good now.

I've received all the pictures you sent me and was so glad to get them. Even the one of Leona Heiden. So Leland is a big shot now? The "big" may be okay but I can think of a better word than shot and it's spelled practically the same.

Dear Folks, Love Orlie

I know that this is pretty short but I'll write again in the next few days. Write often.

Love,
Orlie

Orlie Meskimen

▼

Northern Ireland

July 31, 1942

Dear Folks,

I'll try to write you a few lines tonight. Mainly because I won't be writing much for awhile so don't worry if you don't hear from me on schedule. There are times when it's not possible to write so don't worry – I'm okay.

I got another letter from you today. It was pretty old because it wasn't air mail. Your air mail letters reach me in a period of 8 to 15 days which really isn't so bad considering the distance.

I plan to send some more snaps one of these days. Naturally they will be delayed in reaching you because I won't be able to send them via air mail. Hope you enjoy them. I've received all the pictures you've sent me.

I was rather surprised to hear about Porter and Heiden although I must confess all of the Shellsburg boys over here are glad. It will do both of them a world of good. Jack Peterman too.

I got a letter from Earl Mason also Arline Carroll. She's giving a bunch of girls my address. Earl's a good kid – all of them should be proud of him. If he's ever called he should make an excellent soldier.

Tom, George and I got cigarettes from Rube Senft. Be sure and thank him. I wrote to him and thanked him.

By the way, I raised my allotment to $40 per month. You will receive the first $40 check in October. Also I'm

Dear Folks, Love Orlie

putting between $8 and $15 in savings through the Army over here. You see I draw $79.20 now. It really isn't so bad.

Tom is playing a phonograph we have now. We don't have a radio anymore. He's playing "Concerto for Two" now. Or "Tonight We Love" as it's sometimes called.

Well, folks, I know these letters of mine are awfully brief but I just can't seem to do any better. I think of all of you often though. The picture of you picking berries was very good dad. Made me think of days when we picked them together. Maybe we will next season.

Love,
Orlie

Orlie Meskimen

▼

Northern Ireland
August 11, 1942
Dear Folks,

Received a letter from you today and will try to answer it tonight. Are you able to read these letters when they are typed? If so I'll always type them because it seems like I can get more on these blanks this way. This machine needs a new ribbon. The one in it now is getting bad and doesn't make dark enough letters to really show up good. It's a little Remington portable and really is a nice little machine, but it's been so long since I've typed that is seems like I'm all thumbs. I won't do any paragraphing because I need all the space available to make a decent sized letter. I was rather sorry to hear that LaVonne wasn't able to be up there for the reunion. But then too she might have been a little embarrassed by all the relatives that were there. She will have plenty of time to meet them all in the future.

I have some really good news for you. John Emery is our new first lieutenant. I'm really glad for him because he has waited a long time for something better. He should make a very good leader. Tom is sitting here beside me. He says to tell everyone hello for him. He has a rash of some kind on his arm – nothing really to be alarmed about. He has been kidding me about this typing of mine. Guess he thinks I could be a lot better at this.

We're all well here and in the best of spirits. I

Dear Folks, Love Orlie

haven't received the cigarettes or the other boxes you sent yet but they should be here soon now. I think it would be a good idea if you would insure or register all the boxes you send me. Of course I don't suppose you can insure those you send through the tobacco companies. But the boxes of other things you could. About my Christmas box, just send me a box of the things you think I would like but be sure to send it in time so I can have it to open on Christmas morning. Candy comes through in pretty good shape despite the length of time it takes the boxes to cross. But always send bars that are good and solid. Something like: Clarks, Mars, Babe Ruth's, etc. You can send me a bottle of Vasoline hair oil from time to time though if you like. I like it about the best of any of them. I have a lot of trouble with my hair over here. It gets so dry and we can't buy decent hair oil of any kind here.

Is Russell's little girl as cute as ever? She was surely a cute little thing several years ago. I suppose Marjorie is getting to be a young woman by this time. She surely resembles Dorothy Fogle. Her eyes were exactly like Dorothy's. I suppose the weather is beginning to feel like fall over there by this time. There should be some good squirrel hunting soon now. I wish I could be there to enjoy some of it with Linder. We surely had some good times together. Tell him I said hello and not to shoot off all the squirrels because I'll want a few when next I get home to do some hunting. I imagine Linder will be down by the dump bridge bright and early the first day the season opens.

Orlie Meskimen

That should be either the 15th or the 20th of this month. At least that's when it always did open. Well, I'm about out of room on this paper so I guess I'll have to sign off for this time. I'll try to drop you a line at least once a week. You write to me as often as you can too. Tell everyone hello for all of us and tell them to write to us. At the present we get practically all the news from Shellsburg. I imagine the old burg is getting a little devoid of young men these days.

Love,

Orlie

Dear Folks, Love Orlie

▼

Northern Ireland

August 14, 1942

Dear Folks,

Just a few lines to let you know I'm okay and getting mail from you pretty regularly. I got several letters from you a day or so ago. Also a picture of your porch boxes and Jeep. Everything looked swell but I'd like to have a picture of all the house.

I'll bet the house will look nice when the shingling and painting is done. I think blue trim would look nice. There are so many houses that are trimmed in that color now. This darned pen drops too much ink sometimes.

I am going to give you a list of some things I'd like to have you send me: Vasoline hair oil, cigarettes, gum, air mail stamps and candy. Be sure to send me a carton of cigarettes at least once a month. It will be cheaper if you send the money to the tobacco company and have them send me the smokes. Always send Lucky Strikes.

Our mail gets here pretty good now. We get some mail nearly every day. Your air mail gets here in about 14 days on average. Parcels are a little slow though. I haven't received any cigarettes for several months.

I've had several nice letters from LaVonne recently. She's a darn nice girl. I never realized I liked her so much until I came over here. In every letter she says she's praying for me and that she loves me. Have her up often and get her acquainted with all the relations. It's just possible she might be one of the family some day. At least she will be if I have anything to say about it.

    I guess I'll have to close for this time. I'll write via V-mail in the next few days. Write to me often.

Love,
Orlie

Dear Folks, Love Orlie

Northern Ireland

August 15, 1942

Dear Folks,

Today is Thursday and I'm going to try to write you a few lines with the typewriter on this V-mail blank. I rather imagine this type of mail is the fastest mail we have available. Let me know about how long it takes one of these letters to reach you. We got a little mail today but I didn't get any from you. In fact, I only got one letter and it was from LaVonne. She said that her brother had been home for some time and from the way she talked I guess they surely hated to see him have to return to his outfit. He is an awfully lot like LaVonne and he looks pretty much like her. I met him when I was home on my first furlough. I'm not going to use any paragraphs in this letter because the stationary or forms for this mail is limited so we must use as much of the space as possible. Are these letters pretty easy to read? I'm typing this one because I'm afraid if I write it in ink you won't be able to read it. LaVonne said she wanted to visit you folks but couldn't find any way to get there. I'm sitting pretty good this month as far as the financial end of it goes. I won about 40 pounds in less than a week shooting craps. That's about $165. I plan to bank most of it with the government over here. I guess I told you about the banking system we have over here. Also I told you I had raised my allotment to $40. The first check that you will get for that amount will come from my September pay. I'm banking several pounds over here each month – usually about $15 per month. All in all, I should have a pretty good little nest egg by the time I get home again. A fellow will need all the extra chips he can possibly get his hands on then. I suppose you and the store teeth are getting acquainted by this time, dad? I suppose they were pretty much of a bother at first weren't they? But in the long run you will be much better off. I know I had a couple of bad teeth when we first came over here and as soon as I had them extracted I began to feel better. In fact, I've gained weight since they were pulled. Tom, George and myself are all about the same. We did make a short move but it's nothing to get alarmed about. Tom and I sleep about two beds from each other. We've certainly managed to keep pretty close together since we've been in the service. I'll never regret that I enlisted rather than waited for the draft. I suppose the young fellows are thinning out a lot during these past few months. Did you write that the town of Shellsburg was going to send each of us a carton of smokes each month or did I imagine it? I lost the letter I thought it was in so I couldn't tell for sure. If they do you won't have to send me quite as many cigarettes as I told you to. But you should send me a carton every other month at least. Always send me a little gum each time you send me a package because we aren't able to get any over here and you know I always did chew lots of it. Send me Dentyne. I don't know for sure where Orville Spurgeon is but I have reason to believe he is somewhere near where I am. I've

Dear Folks, Love Orlie

seen Dale Vogt several times just recently though. Tell everyone hello for all of us and tell everyone that would care to write to us. Letters are a nice deal over here even though it is hard to answer them. Our letters probably seem a trifle brief but there just isn't much to write about.

Sincerely,
Orlie

Orlie Meskimen

▼

Northern Ireland
August 19, 1942
Dear Folks,

    I'll try to write you a few lines today. It will necessarily be short but I'll write all I can on this form. I haven't heard from you for a week or so but I'll probably hear from you within the next few days. The last letter I got from you had a picture of Spurgeon's house in it. It surely looked natural. I wrote Clare a letter some time ago.

    I got another carton of cigarettes from the town today but I never seem to get any from you. As long as they send them regularly you won't need to send any or at least quite as often. But do send a box occasionally. They're appreciated more than you will ever know.

    Everything is green and nice over here. I really don't see how grain ever ripens over here but it's getting ripe now. It's mostly rye, wheat and oats. It's so seldom the sun shines and it rains so much I often wonder how it ever keeps from rotting.

    I understand you have already received one of these letters. Hope you are able to read them. Guess I'll have to close – I'm running out of paper and, then too, I've got to write to LaVonne yet today.

Love,
Orlie

Dear Folks, Love Orlie

▼

Northern Ireland

August 31, 1942

Dear Folks,

I am sorry I haven't written for a week or so but circumstances didn't hardly permit. I'll try to write as often as possible though and you do the same. I've had several letters from you the past week or so. Some of them were V-mail. Also I heard from LaVonne, Bernice, Wilma, Don Graham and Anna. I'll try to answer all of them soon. Bernice sent me some nice snaps of herself, Dorothy and the children.

Don wrote me a very nice letter. Said he expected to go soon. I believe he will be alright after he gets acquainted a little. He sent me Arthur's address so I'll drop him a line soon also.

I'll surely be glad to get the box you folks sent me. We aren't able to buy much of that sort of things. Bernice also sent me a box of cigarettes and sweets. You can send me boxes whenever you like. You can use money from my allotment. By the way, starting with my September check the allotment will increase to $40 per month. At that rate I should be able to save a considerable amount by the time I get home. It surely will come in handy though.

We are all well and happy so never worry about us. There will naturally be times when maybe you won't hear from us as often as you'd like but we'll be okay. We do enjoy mail from home so write to us often.

I am sending two more Stars and Stripes today. Of

course, they won't reach you nearly as quick as this letter will. Save them for me. I'll want to take some clippings from some of them.

How does Edna feel about Bob going away? Tell her I said not to worry. I surely wish he could have come with me. I miss him quite a lot even after all this time. It will soon be a year since I was last home. Time passes quickly over here though. It's really hard for me to realize it's nearly fall. It won't be long till it will be good squirrel hunting back there. Wish I could be there to get in on some of it.

Well, I guess I'd better close for this time. Tell Clare "hello" and let him read my letters.

Love,
Orlie

Dear Folks, Love Orlie

▼

Northern Ireland

September 3, 1942

Dear Folks,

Well, another month has passed. It hardly seems as though it should be fall. Of course it really doesn't look like it over here. I suppose the leaves will soon be turning color back there. I'll surely miss the squirrel hunting this fall. I did get to go last fall when I was home on my last furlough.

I've received several letters from you this past week or so. Also some from LaVonne. Most of them were V-mail. Both of you mentioned the fact that LaVonne had been there. I'm surely glad you have such a good time together and that she truly enjoys herself in Shellsburg.

I am going to try to send her a few snaps one of these days. Be sure and send me one of her and Jeep. She thinks he's quite a dog I guess.

I still haven't received your box or Bernice's. But they should arrive soon. I got a nice letter from Rube Senft. He sent me a list of all the fellows from Shellsburg now in the services. The number was rather surprising. Some of them I didn't know had gone.

I got another letter from Reynolds. She's very apologetic these days – says she knows she made a grave mistake. More than likely both of us did but it's all over and done with now. I wrote her a nice letter and told her I would talk to her when I get home. I told her not to write to me anymore because I wouldn't answer her.

Some of us went fishing yesterday and caught 14 perch.

Orlie Meskimen

We just finished eating them. We fried them in butter and were they ever good. Fishing is excellent over here.

    Well, I guess I'd better close for this time. Write me when you can. Also send me more air mail stamps.

Love,
Orlie

Dear Folks, Love Orlie

Northern Ireland

September 5, 1942

Dear Folks,

Just a few lines to let you know I received a letter from you today. It was all about LaVonne's visit. It was the first letter I had received from you in over a week. We get a little mail almost every day though now.

Tom is sitting here beside me writing a letter to his mother. He is pretty elated about her working for Boyer's this winter. Guess he feels maybe she won't be lonesome that way.

By the way, the girl in the picture Tom sent was a perfect stranger to us. We just thought she would make a good picture. She was rather pretty though. Neither of us bother much with the girls over here. I've gone with several but never got really interested in any of them.

Guess this will have to be all for this time. Write when you can.

Love,
Orlie

Orlie Meskimen

▼

Northern Ireland

September 23, 1942

Dear Folks,

    Just a few lines to let you know I'm okay and have heard from you. I received a letter from you today with the pictures in it. Both pictures were very good. Jeepy looked awfully natural. LaVonne looked as if she might be a little bit heavier than when I saw her last. The house certainly looked familiar.

    We have just opened a new recreation house here in camp. We didn't have much to do with it but it's surprising what a nice place we have. There's a library, ping pong tables, books and magazines, and a phonograph. We have an amplifier to govern the volume of the records. Also they send us transcriptions of a lot of the more popular radio programs. The other night we had Bing Crosby, Bob Hope, Gang Busters and Jack Benny. They are having some more tonight but I don't know what they are.

    Well, it looks like I'm running out of paper so guess I'll have to close. I'll write several of these a week. We have to cut down on our air mail considerably. Write when you can.

Love,
Orlie

Dear Folks, Love Orlie

▼

Northern Ireland

September 27, 1942

Dear Folks,

Just a few lines to let you know I've heard from you and that I'm okay. I received the cartons of cigarettes from you and one from Russell. They will surely come in handy. I should receive several more in the next few days. I didn't take my issue cigarettes today because I figured I wouldn't need them. Some of the other fellows can always use them. At the present time I have nearly four cartons so I shouldn't need to worry about having something to smoke for several weeks. But keep sending them because I may not always be so lucky.

You spoke about what I would like in my Christmas box. That's a pretty long story. I'll try to think of the things I would like. Here I go: some nuts, candy, gum, and other things that you think I'd like. Just use your own judgment. Those boxes will have to be mailed in October, just before the first of November if possible. I imagine it will seem rather strange to be sending a box that early. The boxes must not weigh over eleven pounds and not more than one box may be sent by one person per month. I may have to have you give LaVonne the money from my allotment to buy her own present. There's not much I could buy her over here. I know she will understand if I have to do it that way. I get letters from her several times a week. It's awfully hard for me to write very much from over here but I guess she understands that. I try to write her just as often as I do you, but maybe she feels I don't write as much as I should.

Tom and I are sitting here drinking our weekly issue of beer. Which amounts to three cans this week. Most weeks we get a little more than that. It tastes pretty good at that. In fact I'm really beginning to like it. But Tom says to tell you that it doesn't taste as good as we used to drink in Chris's. Maybe someday not so very far distant we'll be back to enjoy some of old Chris's beer with you dad.

I see I didn't get this letter very well centered on the paper but I guess you can read it and that's all that really matters. We are going to have to start using less air mail. So I guess you will be getting more of the V-mail in the future.

I guess from your last letter that LaVonne wasn't able to be in Shellsburg for the reunion. I was rather sorry about that because it would have been a good opportunity for her to meet nearly all my relations. But she might have been a little embarrassed by all the people. She really seems to enjoy visiting you folks. In fact, in every letter she writes to me she mentions you folks.

Well, folks, I guess I'd better close for this time. I'm running out of paper. I'll try to write more the next time. Of course there's only so much room on this paper. Write me whenever you find time. I always enjoy your letters.

Love, Orlie

P.S. Send me some three cent stamps for my Stars and Stripes.

Dear Folks, Love Orlie

▼

Northern Ireland

September 30, 1942

Dear Folks,

Today is our day of rest so I'll write you a few lines. I'm fine and hope all of you are the same. I haven't heard from you for nearly two weeks but I should get a letter in the next few days.

This is the month that you should receive my first $40 allotment. That is, you should get it early in October. Please let me know if it comes through okay. The extra $15 should make my savings mount up pretty fast. Wish I could have made it more. By sending the $40 I still have around $38 to myself. At the present I very rarely go out so I should be able to put some in Soldier's Savings each month. I have around 20 pounds in it now which is about $80.

The weather is pretty cool here these days. It seems somewhat like late October back there in Iowa. The leaves are beginning to change color now. We have had several pretty heavy frosts now.

We received our canteen supplies yesterday so we've been enjoying them today. We got three cans of beer, a carton of cigarettes, two packs of gum, nine candy bars, two cans of fruit juice, and a cigar. This costs us about 8 shillings which is about $1.60 and that really isn't so bad. We always look forward to the day when we're issued our supplies.

Tom and I got a letter from Wes Gillis today. He said he was taking an x-ray course but expected to flunk it so he said he would probably be back at Des Moines. It took us about an hour to read his letter – he's such a terribly poor hand.

    Well I guess I'd better close for this time. I'll write again soon. Don't send anything in my Christmas box that isn't edible unless it would be magazines. Write when you can.

Love,
Orlie

Dear Folks, Love Orlie

▼

Northern Ireland

October 3, 1942

Dear Folks,

I received two letters from you today and was so glad to hear from you. Both of the snaps were very good. I also got a letter from LaVonne.

I was so glad Sergeant Blahnik came to visit you. He was our 1st Sergeant and one of the best in the business. I imagine you had a nice long talk with him. There were four fellows from my outfit that went. I imagine you saw the picture of Corporal Pederson in the Gazette – he was from my outfit too. Sergeant Blahnik promised me he would visit you folks as soon as he got home. I suppose you know he's married and has three children. I'll bet he was glad to get home to see them.

I guess I told you I received your latest box, the one with the candy. I was surely glad to get the stamps today. You won't need to send any more until I tell you to now. I have quite a large number on hand now and I'm going to write more of these letters in the future.

Well, I guess I'll have to close for this time. I'll write a longer letter soon. I was rather surprised to hear about Ray Rubbalty. I suppose he was too old. Write when you can.

Love,
Orlie

Orlie Meskimen

▼

Northern Ireland

October 14, 1942

Dear Folks,

 Just a few lines to let you know I'm okay and I'm thinking of you. I received a letter from you about three days ago along with two snaps. One of the family with Louise and Elmer. Also one of LaVonne.

 The weather over here now is much like it is in Iowa at this time of year. The trees and foliage are rapidly turning brown. There isn't much hunting over here. They do have some pheasants up in the hills. They hunt them in a much different way than we do. They usually go out in groups of about ten. Normally only a few of them carry guns, the rest are "beaters". In other words, they beat the brush and weeds to drive the birds out.

 I got two nice letters from LaVonne. She plans to go to California for a few weeks to visit a friend of hers. I hope she is able to go. The trip will be fun for her and she misses this girlfriend of hers quite a great deal. I suppose you've heard of her – her name is Pat Redmond. LaVonne's brother is still out there too.

 Well, I guess I'll have to close for this time. I'll write more later on. Write when you can. I am going to send a Christmas card soon. It will probably get there long before Christmas but it will be better late than never.

Love,
Orlie

Dear Folks, Love Orlie

Northern Ireland

October 15, 1942

Dear Folks,

    I'll write you a few lines tonight even though I haven't heard from you since I wrote the last letter. In fact, I haven't received any mail for over a week. I haven't received the last box you sent me as yet but should get it soon.

    Things are about the same as usual with us over here. We're all well and happy. Tom is playing pinochle with some of the other fellows tonight. We've all taken to playing a lot of solitaire. Most of the fellows have different ways of playing it so I've learned a lot of new ways.

    I'm doing quite a great deal of reading in the evenings now. I guess I told you about the library we have in camp. I just finished reading "Code of the West" by Zane Grey. I always thought "The Border Region" was the best book he ever wrote.

    If I'm not mistaken I think you misunderstood me about the hair oil. I wanted Vasoline hair oil instead of hair oil and Vasoline. But I guess it will be okay anyway. I'll surely be glad to get those candy bars. You'd better send me more cigarettes about the 15th of next month. If I don't need them I'll try to let you know before then. Maybe I'll have some good news for you one of these days. Guess I'll have to close for this time. Write.

Love,
Orlie

Orlie Meskimen

▼

Northern Ireland

October 21, 1942

Dear Folks,

    I'll try to write you a few lines tonight. I haven't heard from you for several days now. In fact, it's been almost two weeks since last I heard from you. But then the mail hasn't been coming through very good in the last few weeks. I'll try to write one of these letters each week. Occasionally I'll write a long air mail letter too. Did Sergeant Blahnik say anything to you folks about writing to us over here? We haven't heard from any of those fellows since they left us. Some of the fellows are playing the phonograph and they're playing a lot of Bing Crosby records. They surely sound good to me. Most of the records we have are by Bing Crosby, the Ink Spots and the Andrew Sisters. It's really a wonder we haven't worn all the records out by this time. We play the thing from supper until bedtime which sometimes comes pretty late. I got a nice letter from the Davis family. I wrote to them some time ago but I don't know whether or not they got it before they wrote to me. At least they never mentioned it in their letter. I never use paragraphs in these letters because they aren't long enough to write very much on anyway. I suppose they seem rather short to you folks but it's about all I can do to fill one of them let alone writing a long letter. I haven't received the last box you sent me as yet but it surely should be coming through one of these days. We got our canteen supply yesterday and we've been enjoying that. We got 10 cans of beer, 7 packs of cigarettes,

Dear Folks, Love Orlie

candy, gum, cigars, etc. We have a small library here now so I've been doing quite a bit of reading during the evenings. I'm reading a book titled, "Moon Tide" now. It's a pretty good book. By the way, have you noticed the change in my address? I was promoted to First Sergeant just recently. It surely will help me to save a little more money while I'm in the service. I'm going to raise my allotment to something around $75 a month. Did you get the last raise in my allotment this month? You should have gotten it shortly after the first of October. Be sure and let me know if it came through okay. The job I have now is the same job Sergeant Blahnik had before he left us. The weather here remains about the same as it was when last I wrote you. I suppose the weather over there is beginning to get pretty crisp these days. I imagine the pheasant hunting season will soon be in full swing. I believe the season usually opens about the middle of November, doesn't it? Better oil up the old Winchester and head for one of the northern counties this fall dad. You had better have the bolt locking lugs checked on it before using it very much. When I used it last I noticed that the lugs were worn and the bolt refused to lock. It's really rather dangerous that way. It will only cost a small amount to have the lugs replaced. I really believe the Winchester Model 97 is the best shotgun in the business and the safest. When you see Linder tell him I'd surely liked to have been there to help him open the squirrel hunting season down by the dump bridge. I'd almost bet my next check that he was there bright and early the morning the season opened. I suppose Earl Mason comes up to hunt quite often these days. Tell him to take Jeep with him whenever he goes. Well, I guess I'll have to close for this time. I'll write more

Orlie Meskimen

later on. Write me whenever you can. Tell everyone hello for Tom and I. By the way, send me some 3 cent postage stamps in the next letter you write me. I need them to send the Stars and Stripes home. We aren't allowed to send them free anymore. Save all of them for me because I'll want to look through them when I get home. We surely get a bang out of them over here.

Love,
Orlie

Dear Folks, Love Orlie

▼

Northern Ireland

October 26, 1942

Dear Folks,

I still haven't heard from you. It's been over two weeks since last I heard from you. I received a nice letter from LaVonne a couple of days ago though. As you probably know she's in San Francisco now visiting her brother. She seems to be really enjoying herself. Her girlfriend, Pat Redmond, is there too.

Tom got a lot of mail yesterday from home. I believe he got five letters in all. I still haven't got the last two boxes you sent but they should be showing up pretty soon. The letter I got from LaVonne only took ten days to get here and that isn't so bad. I guess she's only going to stay out there for a few weeks. She said she was going to work in some department store while she is there.

I was surprised to hear about Sy Bergen being in the Army. I suppose Don Graham is in now too. As soon as you can, send me his address and I'll try to write him a few lines.

I have a pretty sore arm right at the present. You see, we got some more shots a few days ago and most of our arms got a trifle sore. I got a shot for typhoid and a smallpox vaccination.

Tom is sitting here beside me writing to someone. I imagine it's his mother. He got some pictures from the Boyer family the other day and both of us enjoyed looking at them. I have quite a collection of them that you folks have sent me. LaVonne has sent quite a few too. She surely is good to write to me. As a general rule I hear from her about once a week and sometimes more.

    I seem to be having more trouble writing letters home all the time. It's so awfully hard to think of very much to write. So you'll just have to pardon me if my letters sound quite a lot alike each time I write. At least I'll write once a week to let you know I'm okay even if I can't think of much else to say. Well, it looks as though I have to close for this time. I'll try to write more later. Our mail surely should come through better soon. Write whenever you can.

Love,

Orlie

Dear Folks, Love Orlie

▼

Northern Ireland

October 29, 1942

Dear Folks,

This will be just a few short lines to let you know I'm okay and thinking of you. I received one of the boxes you sent me today and was so glad to get it. It was the one with the candy, gum and hair oil in it. I really wanted Vasoline hair oil but what you sent will do just as well.

The weather here today has been positively lovely. So warm and sunny and that's saying something for this country. It makes me want to get out and go squirrel hunting. The leaves are rapidly falling from the trees and it's beginning to really look like fall now. I'm getting along fairly well with my new job and liking it better every day. I suppose the weather is pretty much like fall back there now. It will soon be time for snow to be falling now. They get very little snow over here.

George King came over the other day and brought us some clippings from the Cedar Valley Times. There was one about Pederson being there to visit all the folks. He was a Corporal in my outfit. I may soon get the same break that Blahnik got.

I saw a pretty good movie the other night in one of our mess halls. We get them usually about once a week but sometimes more. They are up to date pictures so we see them about as soon as they are released. This one was called "Two Yanks in Trinidad".

I forgot to double space this time as you

probably noticed. It's been so long since I did any typing to speak of so I make a large number of mistakes. But I guess you will have a better chance of reading this than you would if I wrote it with pencil or pen. Has John Emery been to see you folks yet?

    Well, I guess I'll soon have to knock off for this time. Maybe I'll be able to write a long letter one of these days. It's really about all I can do to finish one of these V-mail blanks. Write when you can. The mail service hasn't been very good of late but maybe it will soon pick up. Tell everyone hello for Tom and I.

Love,

Orlie

Dear Folks, Love Orlie

▼

Northern Ireland

November 13, 1942

Dear Folks,

I received the first letter I've had in nearly three weeks from you today. I was surely glad to hear from you again after such a long time. I hope it won't be too long a time before I hear from you again. Our mail service isn't a bit better than it was when last I wrote to you. I also got a letter from Arline Carroll in Missouri today. She said that Mary and herself were working at the same place now. She gave my address to a lot of her girlfriends down there. I rather wish she hadn't done that because I have trouble enough writing to the people that are writing to me now.

I don't know whether I told you about me going to officer's candidate school before or not but it's true. I don't know just when it will come but I hope it's soon. It was really better news than being made First Sergeant and that was pretty darned good news.

I suppose Porter was pretty glad to be home on a furlough. It will soon be a year since last I was home. It really doesn't seem like that long a time. I was rather surprised to hear about Bill Reich being over here. Maybe I'll be able to look him up sometime. Shellsburg by this time must be getting pretty devoid of young fellows. I rather imagine Don Graham will pass the examination too. At least there never seemed to be much the matter with him. It will do him good. It's too darned bad that Jack couldn't make it too. I'll never forget the last night Jack and I had in Cedar Rapids. I suppose he's told you all about that long ago.

Tom and I are both well, except for slight head colds occasionally. It is good weather for colds over here now. Colds are pretty common things over here right now. Well, it looks as if I'd soon have to close for this time. I'll be waiting for your letters and also the boxes. Don't go to too much bother with my Christmas box. Make it mostly edibles. Write when you can.

Love,

Orlie

Dear Folks, Love Orlie

▼

Northern Ireland

November 16, 1942

Dear Folks,

I'm sending you these three pictures so I thought I'd write a line along with them. They're really not very good pictures but they'll hold fond memories for me in the future. Some of the fellows in the picture are no longer with my outfit even now. John Emery is standing beside me in the one picture.

We haven't had hardly any mail for over a month. I haven't heard from LaVonne for about three weeks. I got letters from you, Arline Carroll and Earl Mason in this past week though.

By the way, unless you hear differently from me before December 20 I want you to give LaVonne $25 of my money for Christmas. Buy yourselves something too. I'll have to close for this time. Write me when you can.

Love,
Orlie

Orlie Meskimen

▼

Northern Ireland

November 19, 1942

Dear Folks,

This will be just a few lines to let you know I'm okay and thinking of you. I still haven't received much mail from you during the past few weeks. I surely hope the mail service soon picks up again. Nobody has had much mail for well over three weeks. The last letters I got from you were nearly two weeks ago. My letters to you are naturally slowing up a little too because I can't think of much to say when I don't hear from you. I know it isn't your fault but it is hard to write when your letters don't come. I haven't heard much from LaVonne either for about the same amount of time. I surely should be hearing from you soon.

The weather over here goes on about the same. It's very much like autumn in Iowa now. The trees are about all brown now and some of them are bare.

Let me know as soon as Don Graham gets in the Army and I'll write to him. Don should do alright in the Army because I believe he'll like it. Write as many V-mail letters as you can because they're about the only mail that is coming through at all. And even they are pretty slow. I suppose the weather back there is pretty cool these days. The rabbit and pheasant season will soon be in full swing.

Tom got a letter the other day that he couldn't read because it had been wet at some time or other.

Dear Folks, Love Orlie

He couldn't even tell who it was from but thought it was from Boyers. We heard the other day that Minnesota had given Iowa a pretty good trouncing this year in their annual football game. We have about an even mixture of Iowa and Minnesota boys in this outfit so the game has been the main topic in nearly all our conversations the past few days.

Well, it looks as though I'd soon have to sign off for this time. I'll try to write a few of these V-mail letters each week. Write when you can.

Love,
Orlie

Orlie Meskimen

▼

Northern Ireland

November 22, 1942

Dear Folks,

Well, how is everything by this time? I'm well and in the best of spirits. We had our Thanksgiving dinner tonight. It was a little early for Thanksgiving but we enjoyed the meal we had anyhow. We had turkey, dressing, salad, potatoes, gravy, pie, cake and coffee. Not quite as good a dinner as we had last year in Claiborne but a very good one anyway. Then too, conditions are quite different now. They even did a job of decorating in the mess hall. So, all in all, we had a pretty good time and a very good meal.

I still haven't heard from you and I'm beginning to wonder if I ever will again. I'm joking of course but it has been a long time since last I heard from you. There has been a little mail recently but none for me. Maybe I'll get a large amount of it one of these days though.

We are planning a little party here in our unit. We bought a deer from one of the Irish people over here and plan to have it cooked with all the things that go with it. We also plan to have quite a large amount of beer to go with it. So it should be fairly successful. It will be the first party my unit has had since I've been in the Army.

I've written several letters this past week. I wrote to Wilma Narber, LaVonne, Kirk Bixby, Burleys and Earl Mason. I never hear from Wilma anymore so I guess she is probably married by this

Dear Folks, Love Orlie

time. Lots of us are having trouble with colds right now but none of them very serious. I've had one for nearly a week but it doesn't bother me very much. They're just the average head colds we used to have back there. I guess I told you I had raised my allotment to $75 per month. I was glad to hear you had received the $45 okay.

    This typewriter writes so darned faint sometimes but I doubt if you can read it. It needs a new ribbon pretty badly. Write when you can.

Love,
Orlie

Orlie Meskimen

▼

Northern Ireland

November 25, 1942

Dear Folks,

This will be just a few short lines to let you know I received the Christmas box you sent me and that I'm okay. I surely enjoyed the box even though it came a little early. Thanks a million for everything and tell all of the Mason's that I thank them too. I was surely glad to get the watch that they sent me also the handkerchiefs. We can't buy them over here very well because we don't have the ration coupons. I was beginning to get pretty low on them too. I'm sorry I won't be able to send any gifts from over here but it's practically impossible to buy anything over here. By the way, if you get this letter in time only give LaVonne $15 for Christmas. I've been thinking that the former amount that I mentioned was a little too steep. I believe you will understand what I mean.

I was glad to hear you had received the first $45 allotment. Starting the first of December it will raise again, this time to $75. You will get the first installment in January.

The weather is much the same as it has been. I have a minor cold now but it doesn't amount to anything. I suppose you will soon be getting quite a lot of snow. They get a little snow over here but nothing like we do back there. It rarely even stays on the ground long enough for a person to know there has been snow.

I suppose Don Graham is in the Army by

this time. I was rather surprised to hear about Cy Bergen going in the service. Cy will make a very good soldier though because he's already had a lot of training. Has Jack Graham ever been reclassified? He undoubtedly will before so very long. I understand they are starting to do that now. Lots of the fellows that they rejected the first time can be used for something in the service.

Well, it looks as though I would soon have to close for this time. I'll write you an air mail sometime this week. Write when you can.

Love,
Orlie

Orlie Meskimen

▼

Northern Ireland

November 30, 1942

Dear Folks,

    This will be just a few lines to let you know I'm okay and thinking of you. I've received two boxes and about six or seven letters from you in the last few days. I was surely glad to hear from you after such a long break in your letters. Both of the boxes you sent were Christmas boxes and I naturally opened them because I was afraid there would be something in them that would spoil if left too long. I surely enjoyed both of them and want to thank you and everyone else concerned with them.

    I got letters from you, Don Graham, LaVonne, Lois Woodson, Maxson's and Arlene Peterman. Some of them were Christmas cards. Don said he was just as good as in the Army. I rather imagine he will get along okay. I sent you some pictures a few days ago but they won't reach you until after this letter because they are going by a slower mail.

    The weather over here has been about the same as usual. It's rather cool but not as cool as it is over there at this time of year. We had our party the night before last and had a darn good time. The deer we had cooked was swell and everyone seemed to really enjoy themselves. It was the first party this unit has ever had since I've been in the Army. We had all the food and beer that we could use so we had a pretty good time.

    I'll try to write you a long letter via air mail one of these days when I find time and can think

Dear Folks, Love Orlie

of anything to say. It's getting tougher for me to think of anything to say as time goes on. I haven't heard anymore about my going to officer's school but I've passed all the examinations and hope to soon be on my way. Of course, there's a possibility that I'll never get to go but even if I don't I'll still be pretty well off because being First Sergeant pays me $162 a month.

I'm getting along fine so don't worry in any way about me. Tell everyone hello for me and give all the relations my regards. Write when you can.

Love,
Orlie

Orlie Meskimen

▼

Northern Ireland

December 4, 1942

Dear Folks,

I received another letter from you today and was so glad to hear from you. I also got a Christmas box from the town of Shellsburg. Will you thank all those concerned with sending it to me and tell them I sincerely appreciate all they have done since we have been overseas.

The mail service has been much better the past few weeks. We're getting some mail nearly every day now. There was for a long time practically no mail coming over here. I'm glad you liked the Christmas card. I only sent a few. I know I should have sent more of them but they are pretty hard to get and I waited too long before thinking about them.

Has John Emery been up to visit you yet? In the letter I got from you yesterday you mentioned the fact he had been talking to Earl Mason and I naturally supposed he would be up to visit you in the near future. I might possibly get the same opportunity as he did but don't plan on it too much because it might never happen. I sincerely want to go but maybe the quota is full and there is a possibility that they might never call me.

We are all well over here and in the best of spirits. The weather isn't much like Iowa at this time of year. It isn't nearly as cold. Today seems like a day in late September. The trees have all lost their leaves and everything looks pretty bare. It's hard for me to think that it will soon be Christmas time. This past year has surely gone fast for me. It will soon be a year since I was home on my last furlough.

When you find out what Don Graham's address is send it to me. I believe he will like the Army after he's been in awhile and makes a few friends. He's the type that won't have much trouble getting acquainted.

Well, it looks like I'd soon have to close for this time. I'll try to write a bigger letter one of these days when I can think of something to say. Write when you can.

Love,
Orlie

Orlie Meskimen

▼

Northern Ireland

December 8, 1942

Dear Folks,

    This will be just a few short lines to let you know I'm okay and thinking of you. We had a little accident the other night in which Tom was hurt pretty seriously but don't say anything to Mrs. Fish until we see just how he's going to come out. He had quite a large number of bones broken. From all the reports I've received to date he has some broken bones in his chest, some broken bones in his face and a possible skull fracture. They were afraid pneumonia may set in and cause some serious complications. I'm hoping for the best and I guess all anyone can do is just wait and see how it all comes out. I'll take care of all his equipment and see that he gets everything he needs. He probably won't be able to write for some time so you had better talk to Mrs. Fish and tell her just whatever you think you should. I wrote her a letter yesterday and explained it as good as I could without giving her too much cause for worry. I'll keep in touch with you just as I get any news from him.

    The weather over here doesn't change very much as time goes along. It's still very much like early fall back there. I've been getting lots of Christmas cards the past few days. I got a pen and pencil set from Anna Fee the other day. I've lost her address and I guess I'll have to have you send it to me. I'll surely want to thank her for it because

Dear Folks, Love Orlie

I'd lost my fountain pen and I really use one quite a lot too.

I suppose this letter will reach you sometime near Christmas so I'll again wish you a very happy Christmas. It won't be the first Christmas that we weren't together for if you remember I wasn't home on Christmas day of last year. Tell everyone hello for me and wish them a merry Christmas. Let's all hope this thing will be over by next Christmas so we can all be together again. Well, it looks like I'd soon have to close for this time. Write when you can and I'll try to write a little oftener.

Love,
Orlie

Orlie Meskimen

Dec. 10, 1942 – The Regiment moved to England where complete equipment was issued; and passes were issued for London, Manchester and other English cities

———————— ▼ ————————

Somewhere in England

December 18, 1942

Dear Folks,

    This will be just a few short lines to let you know I'm okay and thinking of you. I'm sorry I haven't written sooner but I've been pretty busy these past few weeks. I suppose you've already noticed by my return address that I'm not where I used to be. That's all I can say at the present about it.

    I haven't heard anymore about Tom. He isn't with me anymore, that's the part of the whole accident that I really hate. I suppose we will have to contact each other through you folks at home. I'll try to contact him from over here but I doubt if I will be able to.

    I suppose you have snow there by this time. It hardly seems to me that it will soon be Christmas time. The past year has really flown for me. This time last year I was home on furlough. I'd surely like to be home to get in on a little of the hunting this winter but I guess there will be plenty of time for me to hunt after this is all over. I understand they opened the pheasant season in Benton County this year. I suppose the Army has taken a lot of the annual pheasant hunters away from the States these past few years.

Tell Tom's mother not to worry about him as he will be okay now. I understand they may send him home because he will be physically unfit for the service. I never realized I could miss anyone as much as I miss him. We've been together a long time now. He was closer to me than Bob Bergen ever dared to be.

My examination for officer's school has expired so I guess I'll have to take another in the next few days. They are only good for 60 days and mine has run a little over that. I surely hope I get to go. It won't mean much more money than I'm making now but I'd still like to go.

Well, it looks as though I'd soon have to sign off for this time. I'll write more as soon as I can.

Love,

Orlie

Orlie Meskimen

Dec. 22, 1942 – The Regiment moved to Liverpool and boarded the Empress of Australia the next day

▼

Somewhere

December 25, 1942

Dear Folks,

This will be just a few short lines to let you know I'm okay and thinking of you on Christmas day. I haven't heard from you for about three weeks or a month but then our mail service has been very poor. Maybe it will pick up soon but don't worry because I'm not getting your mail because it's a situation I understand and I know it can't be helped. Maybe you're not getting my mail either so we'll both just have to wait until the service gets better. I'll keep writing though in case it is getting through and you do the same.

We had three pretty good meals today. For breakfast we had stewed prunes, oatmeal, bacon and eggs, marmalade, bread and butter, and of course coffee. For dinner we had turkey, potatoes, baked squash, dressing, bread and butter, marmalade and coffee. For supper we had a tuna salad, assorted cold meats, bread and butter, pie and coffee. So you see we really didn't do so bad, but Christmas dinner at home would have been much better. We all know though that we can't have that until we get this thing over with.

I haven't heard anymore about Tom. I know he's in the hospital but I'm not sure where. I don't

Dear Folks, Love Orlie

think I ever hated anything so much in all my life as I did losing Tom from the outfit. I don't know just how I will get in touch with him again. I wrote to the hospital I think he is in but I'll never know for sure if he is there until I hear from him. From the very latest reports I understand that he has a fractured skull, face and jaw bones broken, and some of his chest bones broken. But I guess he will be okay.

I suppose the hunting is pretty good around Shellsburg now. I'd surely like to be home to get in on some of it. It doesn't even look like we're going to get any snow this winter over here. I haven't seen snow to amount to anything for over two years. There wasn't any at this time last year when I was home. I suppose Jeep does plenty of running around this time of the year. I'll bet he's a pretty good hunting dog by this time. He was about as good as they come when last I took him out. Do you ever take him out dad? Take him with you whenever you go. You'll get more game with him and it's easier. He's darned good running down crippled rabbits.

I've got to have some more dental work done within the next few weeks. I've still got two fillings to be put in. I rather hate to go to the dentist but it looks like I'll have to in order to get my teeth in tip top shape. My teeth are all in pretty good shape except for the two fillings I have to have put in.

Well, it looks like I'd soon have to close for this time. I'm running out of paper and also anything to write. I'll try to write a letter more oftener in the future but it is awfully hard to think of anything to say, even though there is plenty of things I could write but the censors wouldn't pass it.

Tell everyone hello for me and tell them all to write to me as often as they like because I'm always glad to hear from anybody and I'll try to write to them in return. Thank everyone for the Christmas presents they sent me and I'll try to write to them and thank them too. I hope you got the Christmas card I sent you before Christmas. It wasn't very much but it was about as good as I could get over where I was. I haven't received the present LaVonne sent me yet. I'm beginning to think that I never will. Did you send her the money I told you to? By the way, how much money have I at home now? I'd sort of like to know so I will have an idea how I'm coming.

Cheerio for this time. I'll write more next time.

Love,
Orlie

Dec. 25, 1942 – The Regiment sailed for North Africa

Dear Folks, Love Orlie

Orlie at approximately 3 years old

A young Orlie with friends (he is the blond boy in the center)

Orlie Meskimen

Orlie with his dog Pal, 1931, 12 years old

A young Orlie

Dear Folks, Love Orlie

A teenage Orlie with his mother Clara

A teenage Orlie with his mother Clara

Orlie Meskimen

Orlie is 2nd from left; his father Roy is 3rd from right in background

Basketball 1935

Basketball 1936

Dear Folks, Love Orlie

Orlie with his loving parents

Orlie's dog Jeepy; photo captioned "Jeep: Boss of the ranch"

Orlie's senior class photo, Shellsburg High School

Orlie Meskimen

Orlie at Camp Claiborne

Orlie with a group of fellow soldiers (Orlie is far right)

Orlie with dog at Camp Claiborne

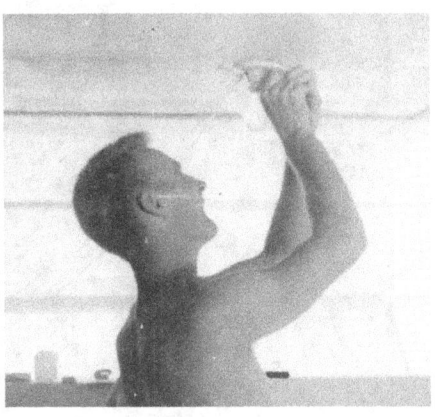

Orlie at Camp Claiborne, captioned "This is a lousy picture. One of the fellows snapped it of me when I was fixing my light. You can see my 'Butch' haircut though."

Orlie wearing the helmet that saved his life

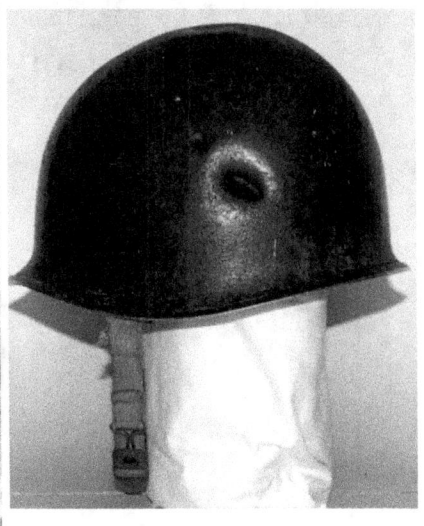

Photo of the helmet that saved Orlie's life when he was hit by shrapnel behind his left ear at Monte Cassino

Orlie Meskimen

Orlie enjoying a cigar with friends Corp. Dick Emery (center) and Sgt. Harvey McDougle (right), as mentioned in letters dated May 13, 1943 and October 23, 1944. Sgt. McDougle was killed in action.

Shellsburg Man Security Chief On Isle of Guam

SGT. MESKIMEN

SHELLSBURG — First Sgt. Orlie Meskimen, son of Mr. and Mrs. C. L. Meskimen of Shellsburg, has been made chief of the security branch in the corps of engineers for the whole of the island of Guam, according to information received by his parents here.

Sgt. Meskimen is the first enlisted man to hold this position. It formerly was in the hands of a civilian.

During the war, the sergeant served in Italy. After the end of hostilities, he took special instruction which fitted him for his work in the security section.

The Shellsburg man has been in Guam about two years. He is expected home in March for a visit. During the time he is in the States, he will take more specialized training, his parents have been notified.

Newspaper article announcing Orlie's appointment as chief of the Corps of Engineers security branch for the island of Guam

Dear Folks, Love Orlie

Orlie at the Presidio, San Francisco, CA, January 1950 (Second Relief, Company A, 701st Military Police Battalion)

-- Shellsburg, Iowa, honor roll list of veterans

Orlie Meskimen

Orlie hunting with a friend

Orlie's mother Clara and father Clifford "Roy"

Dear Folks, Love Orlie

Orlie's mother Clara holding flowers he sent her; photo is captioned "Orlie, this was taken May 10, 1942 on Mother's Day, With all my love, Mom"

Orlie's maternal grandmother May; photo is captioned "Orlie, this picture of grandma was taken right after she was sick. She looks lots better now"

Orlie Meskimen

Orlie's future wife LaVonne Butler

Orlie's future wife LaVonne Butler with her brother Bernard

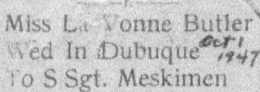

Miss LaVonne Butler Wed In Dubuque *oct 1 1947* To S Sgt. Meskimen

Announcement is made of the marriage of Miss LaVonne Butler, daughter of Mrs. Mary Butler of Anamosa to S Sgt. Douglas Meskimen, son of Douglas Meskimen of Shellsburg, Iowa.

The ceremony was read Wednesday at Dubuque, Iowa.

Attending the couple were Mrs. Pat Hogan of Anamosa and Earl Mason of Shellsbug.

The bride wore a brown suit with matching accessories and an orchid corsage. Mrs. Hogan wore navy blue with a pink hat and matching accessories. Her corsage was of baby's breath and carnations.

Earl Mason of Shellsburg attended the groom as best man.

The wedding party was entertained at a dinner Wednesday evening at the home of the bride's aunt in Cedar Rapids.

Mrs. Meskimen has been employed the past few months at Wolfe's Cafe. S Sgt. Meskimen is with the Civil Investigation Department of the Army. Following the wedding trip to San Francisco, Calif. he will leave for duty in Guam.

Orlie's future wife LaVonne Butler

Newspaper announcement for the marriage of Orlie Meskimen and LaVonne Butler

Dear Folks, Love Orlie

Orlie and LaVonne on their wedding day (Orlie's mother Clara Mason-Meskimen is far left; LaVonne's mother Mary McCardle-Butler is far right)

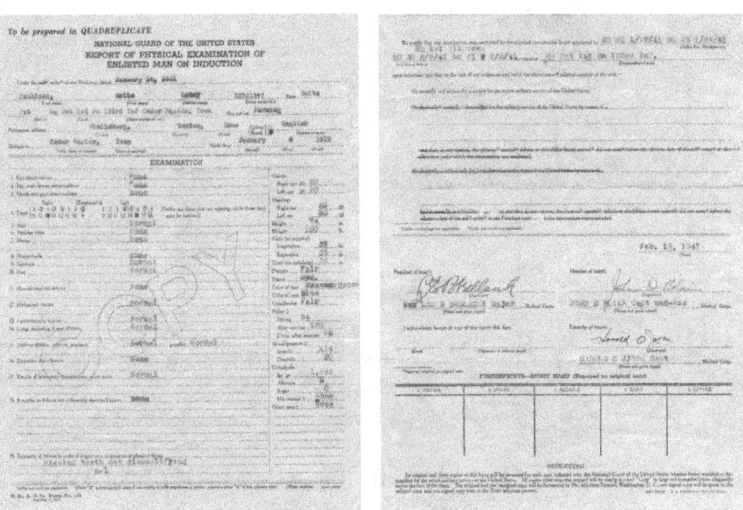

Orlie's physical examination record upon enlistment

Orlie Meskimen

Separation Qualification Record issued July 6, 1945

Dear Folks, Love Orlie

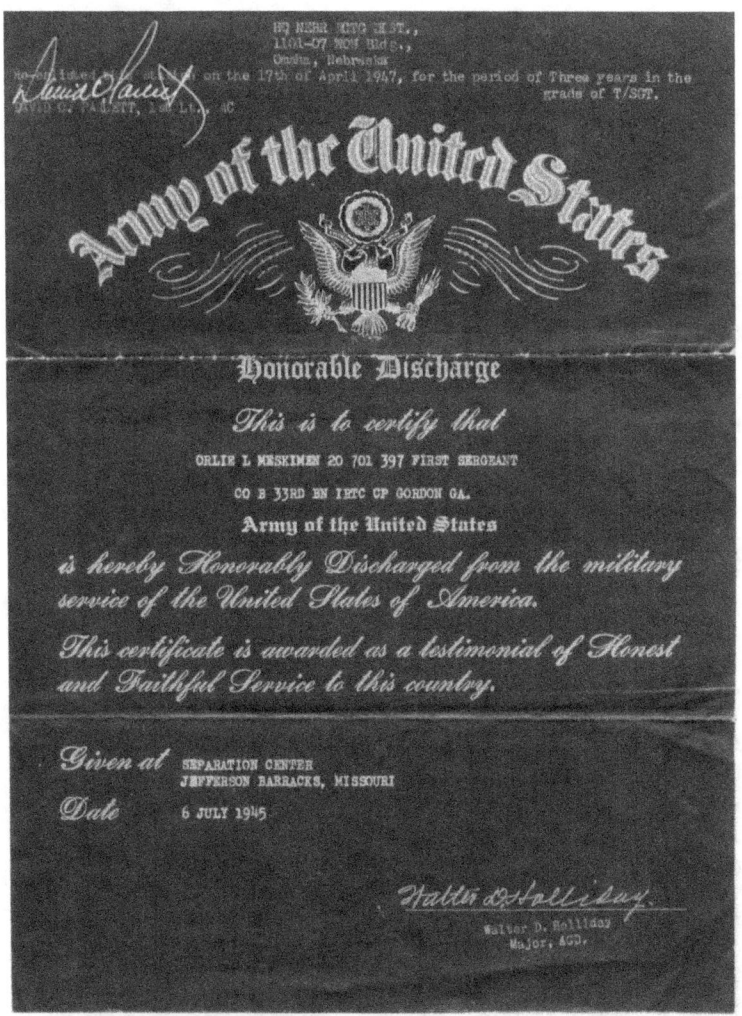

Honorable discharge certificate issued July 6, 1945; states that Orlie re-enlisted April 17, 1947, for a period of three years

Orlie Meskimen

Second page of Honorable Discharge Certificate issued July 6, 1945

Dear Folks, Love Orlie

Honorable discharge paper issued November 29, 1949; states that Orlie re-enlisted at the Presidio of San Francisco on November 30, 1949, in grade of Sergeant First Class to serve for an unspecified period

Orlie Meskimen

Army of the United States
SEPARATION QUALIFICATION RECORD
SR 600-480-1

This summary of preservice experience and military qualifications is given to personnel upon separation from the service. The information contained hereon was taken from Army records and supplemented by a personal interview. The purpose of the record is to aid in appraising the individual's qualifications for civilian employment or schooling. It may be presented to prospective employers, representatives of schools or used in any way that will assist the individual in making a suitable civilian employment adjustment.

1. NAME AND SERVICE NUMBER	2. DATE OF BIRTH			3. MARITAL STATUS	4. DEPENDENTS		
Meskimen, Orlie L RA 20 701 397	Day 6	Month Jan	Year 19	Married	Spouse 1	Children 1	Other 0

5. HOME ADDRESS (No. and Street or RFD, City and State)	6. LENGTH OF SERVICE	7. NAME AND ADDRESS OF LAST EMPLOYER
Shellsburg, Iowa	Yrs. 10 Mos. 3 Days 26	Iowa Canning Company, Vinton, Iowa

8. CIVILIAN EDUCATION

GRAMMAR AND HIGH SCHOOL (Circle highest grade completed)	COLLEGE OR UNIVERSITY	Year Left School	High School Specialty
1 2 3 4 5 6 7 8 9 10 11 (12) GRAD X	1 2 3 4 GRAD 5 6 7	1937	Vocational

	Name and Location	Major or Specialty	Degree	Year
COLLEGE OR UNIVERSITY	None			
POST GRADUATE	None			

TRADE, VOCATIONAL, BUSINESS AND CORRESPONDENCE COURSES			Completed	
School	Courses Taken	Duration	Yes / No	Year
None				

Apprenticeship	Formal / Informal
None	

9. RECORD OF CIVILIAN EMPLOYMENT

From	To	Type of Job	From	To	Type of Job
1945	1947	Foreman (Labor)			

10. MAIN CIVILIAN OCCUPATION

Title of Position	Months Held	DOT Code Number
Foreman (Labor)	18	5-90.000

Duties Performed: Worked as foreman in a vegetable canning plant. Supervised the work of about forty (40) men, also trained new employees, directing work, assigning jobs and keeping production up to standards.

11. SECOND BEST CIVILIAN OCCUPATION

Title of Position	Months Held	DOT Code Number
Machine Operator	36	5-78.000

Duties Performed: Operated a machine which tightened and loosened bolts a rail joints.

12. OCCUPATIONAL LICENSE OR CERTIFICATE HELD	13. AVOCATIONS AND HOBBIES
None	Hunting(12 guage shotgun)

14. LANGUAGES (Specify)	understands Exc./Good/Fair	Reads Exc./Good/Fair	Writes Exc./Good/Fair	15. SPORTS (Specify)	Amat.	Prof.	Coach
(1) None				(1) Basketball	X		
(2)				(2)			
(3)				(3)			

DA FORM 493 (1 Nov 52)

1st page of Separation Qualification Record issued February 2, 1953

Dear Folks, Love Orlie

16.	MILITARY EDUCATION			
Title of Course	Description		Name of School	Weeks
(1) Investigations	Criminal Investigation		TMPS-Carlisle Barracks, Penn	6
(2)				
(3)				

17. PRINCIPAL MILITARY DUTY ASSIGNMENTS			
Duty Assignments	Months	Duty Assignments	Months
Military Police	30		
Administration Specialist	30		

18. MAIN MILITARY DUTY ASSIGNMENT			
Title of Position	MOS Code	Grade Held	Months
Administration Specialist	1502	M/Sgt	30
Duties Performed: Supervised all administrative details for Post Adjutant.			
Tools and Equipment Used: General Office Supplies and typewriter		Supervisory Responsibilities: Supervise 15 clerks.	

19. SECOND BEST MILITARY DUTY ASSIGNMENT			
Title of Position	MOS Code	Grade Held	Months
Military Police	1677	Sfc	30
Duties Performed: Desk Sergeant...Dispatched all patrols for post. Used voice radio to give orders. Maintain desk blotter.			
Tools and Equipment Used: Voice Radio and General Office Supplies		Supervisory Responsibilities: Supervised 30 men.	

20. QUALIFIED TO OPERATE: [X] Automobile [X] 2½ Ton Truck [X] Other wheeled vehicle

21. ADDITIONAL INFORMATION
Remarks: None

22. MILITARY OBLIGATIONS AFTER SEPARATION
Exempt from induction except after a declaration of war or national emergency

23. STATEMENT AND SIGNATURE	24. SIGNATURE OF SEPARATION OFFICER
I have read and consider the above information a true summary of my civilian and military experience and training.	Date: 2 Feb 53 — Signature
Signature and Grade	Typed Name, Grade and Title: JOHN L. TOOMEY CWO USA

2nd page of Separation Qualification Record issued February 2, 1953

Orlie Meskimen

ARMY SERVICE FORCES
SIXTH SERVICE COMMAND
FORT SHERIDAN, ILLINOIS

Reception Station #7

MESKIMEN, ORLIE L.   20 701 397

I certify that _____
is authorized to wear the following ribbons and decorations:

American Defense Service Ribbon

Good Conduct Ribbon

EAME Theatre Ribbon

~~Asiatic-Pacific Theatre Ribbon~~

~~American Theatre Ribbon~~

Three Bronze Battle Stars

~~Air Medal~~

~~Oak Leaf Clusters~~

Combat Inf Badge

R. E. Worzella
R. E. WORZELLA,
1st Lt., A.U.S.
Ass't Adjutant.

Statement of ribbons and decorations awarded to Orlie including three bronze battle stars

Dear Folks, Love Orlie

Sample of Camp Claiborne letterhead #1

Sample of Camp Claiborne letterhead #2

Sample of Camp Claiborne letterhead #3

Sample of Camp Claiborne letterhead #4

Orlie Meskimen

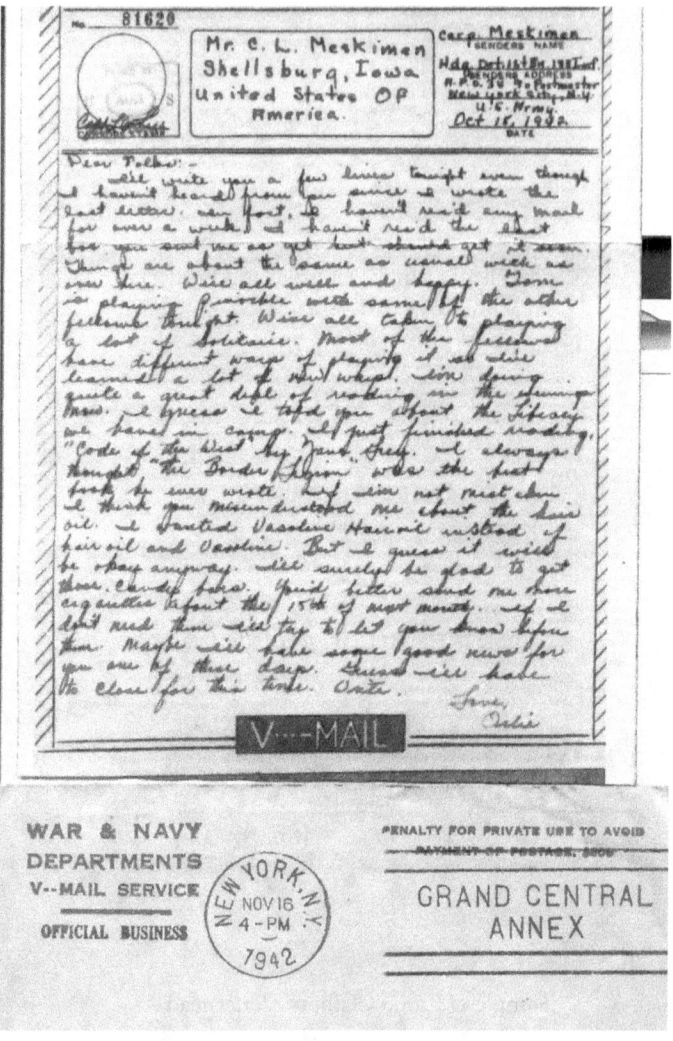

Sample of "VMail" (V-mail, short for Victory Mail, was a hybrid mail process used by America during the Second World War as the primary and secure method to correspond with soldiers stationed abroad. To reduce the cost of transferring an original letter through the military postal system, a V-mail letter would be censored, copied to film, and printed back to paper upon arrival at its destination)

Dear Folks, Love Orlie

Sample of Orlie's letter where specific words were censored

Orlie Meskimen

Article that appeared in the Milwaukee Journal Sentinel December 29, 2010.

JANUARY 1943
NORTH AFRICA

Jan. 3, 1943 – The Regiment landed at Mers El Kabir (Oran) after a voyage climaxed by the Empress being rammed by another ship of the convoy, and marched to Assi Ben Okba, ten miles East of Oran. A period of light training, guard duty, and passes to Oran followed.

▼

Somewhere in North Africa

January 7, 1943

Dear Folks,

This will be just a few short lines to let you know I've changed my address. I shouldn't say address but location. I'm now in North Africa. It's quite a change from anything I ever saw before. I'll tell you all I can about it. The people are nearly all French, Spanish or Arabic. There are none or very few who speak English. Everything in general reminds me of the way they live in Mexico. We are using French money – it's about 75 Francs to the dollar. There's nothing much we can buy so there's little use for money. I raised my allotment to $100 per month and I'll put around $40 more in Solder's Savings each month. That will leave me about $26 which should be plenty. The Soldier's Savings pays off when I get my discharge or to you if anything happens to me.

There are some very strange customs here. There are quite a large number of Arabs who believe in the Mohammed religion. The women wear veils and have crosses tattooed on their foreheads and chins. They consider it a very great sin to even look at these women. A great many of them believe that souls of former Arabs are in snakes, so we were cautioned never to kill a snake where an Arab can see us. Tangerines and oranges are abundant and can be bought very reasonably.

It looks very much as though my officer's training is out of the question now. I was all set to go but it just can't be helped now. John was lucky to get to go when he did. I'm making pretty good money though, so I'll still be able to save quite a little.

Yesterday, as you know, was my birthday. It was the second away from home. The years surely go fast in the Army. Maybe by this time next year I'll be home again. I'll surely have some great experiences to tell you. I've done quite a good deal of traveling since I've been in the service, haven't I?

We've got quite a lot of mail these past few days. I've had letters from you, LaVonne, Diane, Jack Graham, Kirk Bixby, Jack Peterman. Cards from Burley's, Edaburns,

Dear Folks, Love Orlie

Maxson's. Most of it was November mail – that accounts for the lack of mail when we were in the other place. Well, I guess I'll have to close for this time. Write when you can and I'll do the same. Sometimes my letters may not come for long periods of time but don't worry – I'll be okay.

God bless all of you.
Love,
Orlie

Orlie Meskimen

▼

North Africa

January 19, 1943

Dear Folks,

    Received your V-mail of December 28 today and was so glad to hear from you. It was the first letter I've had from you in some time. Our mail service should pick up soon though. I'm getting along fine down here. We're all beginning to acquire suntans. The sun is pretty hot during the days but the nights are really cool. The weather is much better than it was where we were before. We take off our shirts for a short time each day and in the heat will get a good tan without overdoing the job. I was glad you sent LaVonne the $25. Hope she was able to get something she wanted with it. I got a letter from her about two days ago. Write to me by mail all the time. You've probably heard about the new postal regulations concerning mail to the fellows overseas. Air mail is no good whatsoever. I'll try to write once or twice a week but there may be times when I won't be able to write quite that often. If so, please don't worry – it's just that I'll be busy. Write when you can. Tell everyone "hello" for me.

Love,
Orlie

Dear Folks, Love Orlie

▼

North Africa

January 31, 1943

Dear Folks,

This will be just a few short lines to let you know I'm okay and thinking of you. I haven't heard from you for about a week but the mail service is getting fairly good again so the letters should begin to come through. I got three letters today. One from LaVonne, one from the Mason's and one from Uncle Burley. I also got a carton of cigarettes from a Mrs. L. P. Suits. I can't seem to think who that could be. My only guess is that it's LaVonne's mother. If it's someone you know thank them for me and tell me who it is so I can write to them myself. I've wracked my brain and I'll be darned if I can think who it could be. LaVonne has a step father though and that could be his name. It kind of seems like it was.

The last letter I had from you was the one in which you mentioned about my allotment money not coming through as it should. I really can't understand why it shouldn't come through as per schedule. You should have gotten $40 for the months of September, October and $75 starting the first of either November or December – I'm not sure which. By all means write and see if you can find out why it didn't come in that manner. I'm going to start sending money home via money order as soon as we get paid again. There's really no use for very much money down here.

The Mason's mentioned the fact that people know about Tom getting hurt back there now. I wrote to Mrs. Fish so she wouldn't worry too much if she didn't hear from

Orlie Meskimen

Tom for a period of time. I knew he was pretty badly hurt and might not be able to write for quite some time. I wrote him a letter since I've been down here but don't know just how long it will take it to reach him.

LaVonne sent me some very nice pictures of herself and her mother. She's certainly very good about writing. I hear from her quite often. Think I just have made a hit with her. She worries quite a lot about her brother. It seems she hasn't heard from him since he left the states. Sometimes it takes a long time for a fellow to get settled to the extent that he can write letters. It depends a lot on what his quarters are like and if he has the necessary stationary available. It doesn't pay to worry too much in times like these.

Rationing must be beginning to tighten down over there according to the letter the Mason's wrote me. Bessie was stating all the various commodities they had to account for in their monthly reports. According to her the gas situation must be getting rather acute by this time. I don't suppose you folks are able to get very much, are you? I can readily understand where all the gas is going.

Burley wrote to say that Carl is married. I believe he's about two years younger than me, isn't he? It's been so long since I saw any of the relatives to speak of that I forget ages and faces pretty easily. Diane wrote that Louise had had her baby and that Marion Reynolds was her nurse. It was the first that I knew of the incident.

Well, it looks as if I'd soon have to close for this time. My letters are awfully short but I just can't seem to think of very much to say. This machine works so poorly that its getting to be more bother than good. Write when you can.

Love, Orlie

Dear Folks, Love Orlie

Feb. 1, 1943 – The Regiment assembled in the vicinity of Lavayssiere

▼

North Africa

February 4, 1943

Dear Folks,

We finally got a large amount of mail. I got about 12 letters from you in one day. That was the day before yesterday. All in all, I got about 25 letters. I surely enjoyed reading them. It took nearly all day for me to read them.

I was surely glad to hear Tom was okay and that you had heard from me since I've been down here. I believe the mail service will be better from down here. I'll write as often as I can but there may be times when I'll be too busy. No doubt you can guess what I'm doing. I wish Tom would write soon. I wrote to him soon after I got here.

I got letters from you, LaVonne, Claude Blattler, Maxson's, Uncle Fred, Dorothy and Bernice. Christmas cards from you, the Iowa Canning Company, Uncle Clarence, a couple of girls in Ireland, and LaVonne. I haven't received the picture or the birthday cable from LaVonne. She sent me some nice snaps in one of her letters. I surely enjoy all the snaps she sends.

There is no way I can check up on my allotment from over here. All I know is that they took the money out. They've taken $75 out for December and January. You should receive that okay. I think I will raise it to $100. I really don't need much money down here. I also plan to get $10,000 insurance.

Orlie Meskimen

I am enclosing a snap of myself sitting by my "pup" tent. There is a raincoat full of tangerines beside me. All of us have short haircuts as you can see. My hair is only about an inch long. It was an order that we get it cut short. It feels much better and is so much easier to take care of.

I was supposed to forward all of Tom's mail for him but I have a corporal doing it for me. He still gets quite a lot of mail down here. I suppose they will get it straightened out soon.

I'll try to explain a little more about my promotion. You see, I am the highest rank a man can be without being an officer. They run in this manner: Private, Private First Class, Corporal, Sergeant, Staff Sergeant, Technical Sergeant, First or Master Sergeant. I was surely disappointed when I didn't get to go for officer's training but maybe it just wasn't to be.

The outfit has changed an awfully lot. There are hardly any of the old gang left. Lots of the boys are easterners now. I have about 120 men under me now. And I'm short some too. George King is still a Sergeant. He and Olson are the only Benton County boys left.

I suppose "Jeep" would like to go hunting these days. He's liable to be all over his hunting days before I get home again.

Well, it looks as though I'd soon have to close for this time. It's awfully hard for me to think of anything to say. But, I'll surely have some great experiences to tell you about when I get home again. Write when you can.

Love,
Orlie
PS. Tell everyone "hello" for me.

> Feb. 7, 1943 – The Regiment moved by truck over the bitter cold Atlas Mountains to the vicinity of Maktar, preparatory to relieving the French units in sector south of Fondouk Pass and east of Hadjeb-el-Aioun
>
> Feb. 17, 1943 – The 3rd Battalion made contact with advancing elements of Romel's [sic] 21st Panzer Division and stopped them. The same day the 1st Battalion was equally successful in turning back the enemy at Kef-el-Amar Pass. Ordered to withdraw the next day.

▼

North Africa

February 24, 1943

Dear Folks,

This will be just a few short lines to let you know I'm okay and thinking of you. No doubt you wonder why you haven't heard from me for quite awhile. I've been on the front so I haven't been able to do any writing. I'll write whenever I can though so please don't worry about me.

We got a little mail today. I got six letters – three from you, two from LaVonne, and one from Clare. Yes, it's true about Woodson being here but I haven't seen him yet. I haven't seen King for nearly three weeks. He's a clerk you know. Joe Timmins and Dick Emery are both with me.

All your letters sound as if it was pretty cold in Iowa now. I suppose the hunting season is about over with. I was rather surprised to hear about Earl Mason being in the Army but they soon grow up when one is gone for a few years. I've never heard from Tom yet but I wrote him one letter. It probably took it quite some time to reach him.

I got LaVonne's picture several days ago. It is a very good picture but it's rather hard to carry. At the present I'm carrying it inside my shirt.

It's awfully hard to think of much to write about. There's so little I can say. There isn't anything I need. We get all the cigarettes we need and also food. Our cigarettes are free ration now.

I suppose the old "Burg" is about the same. Must not be many of the young fellows around. I got a letter from Kirk Bixby about a month ago. He said he sure wished he could be in too. That burns me plenty because there's sure as hell nothing stopping him. I never could figure out why Wayne Boyer and him were never drafted.

Well, it looks like I'd soon have to close. Write when you can – our mail is coming through no matter where we are. Take care of yourselves. Take care of my guns, dad, I'll be wanting them next fall. I'll write again when I get time.

Love,
Orlie

Dear Folks, Love Orlie

March 11, 1943 – 1st Battalion recaptured Kef-el-Amar Pass with heavy losses in Company

▼

North Africa

March 16, 1943

Dear Folks,

This will be just a few short lines to let you know I'm okay and thinking of you. I haven't heard from you for quite some time but maybe the mail service will get better as time goes on.

As you already know, I'm not writing very much but it's because I've been on the front. I've spent a lot of time digging "fox holes" and find it pays really great dividends. We have a saying that there's no such thing as an atheist in the fox hole and I can readily assure you it's true. I'm not getting along as bad though so don't worry about me. We get pretty good food and all the cigarettes we can smoke. The only thing we really want is lots of mail so write lots of letters and perhaps they will reach me sometime.

I suppose that by the time you get this letter the farmers will be sowing oats around there. It hardly seems as though it should be that time of year. Time surely flies for me. We haven't been paid for nearly three months now. The last money I had was for December. Write and let me know how my allotment money is coming through. I have $10,000 insurance now. I also sent $20 home yesterday. Use it for something around the house or something else you might need.

Orlie Meskimen

Well, it looks as though I'd soon have to close for this time. I'll write again as soon as I can. I wrote to LaVonne last week. We write one letter each week. I understand we are supposed to get some mail in the next few days so maybe I will get some letters from you then. I haven't heard from LaVonne for nearly a month. Not since before I got her pictures. Write when you can. Give my regards to everyone.

Love,
Orlie

Dear Folks, Love Orlie

▼

North Africa

March 19, 1943

Dear Folks,

I received two letters from you folks yesterday. One from Grandma and one from mother. Both of them were fairly recent letters. I got a total of nine letters. Two from you, one from LaVonne, Dorothy, Bernice, Russell, the Maxson's, Marlene Buettner (Koopman), and Clare. It will be quite a while before I will ever get them answered. We're only allowed one letter per week so it's pretty hard to answer all the letters. I'm writing two today because of this money order I'm enclosing. I want you to use it for anything you might need around the house. I thought of sending it to LaVonne but decided that since spring is coming I thought you would be able to use it around the house.

Everything is going about the same with me. I'm well and in the best of spirits. There really isn't anything you could send me that would help. I get everything I need. Just write lots of letters and give me all the news around the old "Burg".

I surely hope the picture LaVonne is having enlarged turns out okay. It was taken where I was before just a few days after I was made First Sergeant. I really can't remember just what the picture looked like.

Well, folks, I'll have to close for this time. I'll write more next time. I've a little work to do now. Write when you can.

Love,
Orlie

Orlie Meskimen

▼

North Africa

March 25, 1943

Dear Folks,

Today is our day to write again so I'll drop you a few lines during the noon hour. I wrote to LaVonne last time. I try to alternate between the two of you. We've had lots of mail from home during the last week or so. I got one letter from LaVonne written just after she had been to Shellsburg to visit you folks. She said she had a very nice time and surely enjoyed being with you folks. I suppose you know she is going to California for the duration. She assured me she would be in Cedar Rapids when I got home again. Guess she figured I might decide to stop writing.

Everything is okay with me. There are all kinds of wild flowers starting to bloom here now. Most of them are the types of flowers that grow around rocks and sand. I notice there is one species I have in my rock garden. It's that pale green plant that spreads so much. Most of the flowers are small and very delicate. Sure will be nice to be home working on the rock garden in the evenings.

I suppose the weather is beginning to look more like spring there every day now. The weather here compares with July in the daytime back there and October at night. The sun tans or burns one so fast that it's practically dangerous to go about with exposed skin for any length of time. But the sun surely feels good – for such a long time we rarely saw the sun.

Well, it looks as though I'd soon have to close for this

Dear Folks, Love Orlie

time. I'll write again soon. I'm sending you the duplicate copy of my insurance application. Write when you can.

Love,
Orlie

Orlie Meskimen

▼

North Africa

March 31, 1943

Dear Folks,

This will be just a few short lines to let you know I'm okay and thinking of you. I haven't had any mail for about a week but will probably get some in the next few days. I believe the mail service will be pretty good now. I've received letters from you written as late as March 11th, so you can see it isn't so bad.

Things are about the same with me. I've had a slight skin infection on my face but it's healing up now. I believe it was caused by something biting me. Outside of that I can't complain very much.

I was glad to hear the allotments are straightening out. You should get $70 for one or two months and from there on it will be $100. I haven't been paid since I was paid for December so I've quite a little coming. As soon as they pay us again I'll send nearly all of it home by money order. For the three months back I'll draw $496.80. Of course, you will get $300 via allotment and I'll send at least $175 more. My victory tax and income tax will cost me about $260 per year so it will really cut into my savings.

I haven't heard from LaVonne since she went to California, but no doubt I will in the near future. I've surely had a lot of letters from her so far this month.

It's hard to realize tomorrow will be the first of April.

Dear Folks, Love Orlie

Time surely flies for me over here. It will be winter time again before we know it. Surely hope I'm able to do some hunting in Iowa this next winter. I got a letter from Linder sometime ago and he said he hadn't killed all the game around there yet.

Well, it looks like I'd soon have to close for this time. Write when you can.

Love,
Orlie

Orlie Meskimen

▼

North Africa

April 5, 1943

Dear Folks,

I have a few moments before making some of my reports so I will write you a few lines. I got my first letter from Tom today since we were separated. He is with a new unit so I guess we will have to wait until this is over with before we meet again.

In answer to your question about whether I go to the front or whether I stay behind and do book work, I'll say this. It's a combination of the two. I have been on the front. That's about all I can say about what I'm doing.

I suppose the weather there now is very much like spring. It won't be long now until the farmers will be working in the fields in earnest.

I was rather surprised to hear about Ted Emler and some of those older fellows being called for the draft. I hardly thought they were drafting men that old – especially married men. I haven't heard of Orville Spurgeon being here yet but it's easy to understand why I wouldn't hear about him. I haven't seen Woodson since we came here either.

It looks as though I'd soon have to close for this time. I'll write more as soon as I can. Sometimes there may be quite long periods of time between my letters but don't worry. Write when you can and take care of yourselves. I got a letter from Marjorie Graham a few days ago. She said she was graduating from High school this spring. It's hard to believe she's that old.

Love, Orlie

Dear Folks, Love Orlie

> April 8, 1943 – Battle for Fondouk Pass began in a bitter struggle for hill 306, with the 1st Bn. finally storming and clearing it two days later.
> April 10-25, 1943 – The Regiment trained intensively around Fondouk, then Makatar.

------▼------

Tunisia

April 14, 1943

Dear Folks,

It's been nearly a week since last I wrote you but I've been busy again so didn't have time to write. You undoubtedly know I'm in Tunisia now. In fact, I have been for quite some time. But I guess you know about everything I know.

The weather here has been very warm. I've had some trouble with my hands and face chapping. After the two shots of sun stroke I had I sort of figured the African sun would get me down but it hasn't bothered me very much yet. I had a lot of trouble at Claiborne but I guess I must have overcome all that old trouble.

The last letter I had from you was post marked March 24th. All in all, our mail service has been pretty good. I understand our mail to you makes pretty good time too. I've had letters from the Popenhagens, Socks, LaVonne, Diane, Marlene Buettner, and Tom. Tom wrote to me from England. He seemed well satisfied. He is much better off where he is than he would be down here.

I think I will be able to write more often from now on. For awhile we were restricted to just a couple of letters each

Orlie Meskimen

week. I just finished one to LaVonne and I've several more I must write during the next few days.

Well, I guess I'll have to close for this time. I'll write more in the next few days. Write when you can.

Love,
Orlie

Dear Folks, Love Orlie

▼

Tunisia

April 23, 1943

Dear Folks,

Thought I would drop you a few lines today while I had a little time. I got two letters from you yesterday and was so glad to hear from you. I am sitting under some cork trees writing this letter. The Arabs use the cork for fuel. Nearly every tree has been stripped for as high as they can reach. There is so little wood for fuel that I guess they're glad to get anything.

I ran into Homer Woodson a few days ago and he was still okay. Guess he had some pretty exciting times just as I have had. He lost all his personal belongings in one deal.

I imagine everything is beginning to look like spring back there now. It hardly seems possible that it will soon be the 1st of May. The months surely fly by for me over here.

I put $270 in soldier's savings a few days ago. It will draw .03% interest and I will get it along with my discharge. It will just about pay my income tax for this year. Don't know what I owe for last year.

I also got letters yesterday from Clare, Tom and a girl where I was before. The letter I got from Tom was an old one written before the one I got last. I guess I'll have to close for this time. I'll write again soon. Write when you can. I don't believe very much of your mail to me has been lost – just a little late.

Love, Orlie

April 29, 1943 – The Regiment moved to Sidi Nsir in sight of the Mediterranean, and joined in the bitter three day struggle that ended in the capture of hill 609. The 1st Bn. made the final and successful attack while under the command of the 135th Infantry.

May 2-8, 1943 – The Regiment participated in the battles for Eddekhila and Chougui Pass over mountainous terrain where supply was the greatest problem.

▼

Tunisia

May 3, 1943

Dear Folks,

Just a few lines to let you know I'm okay and thinking of you. I'm in the hospital now but it's nothing serious so don't worry. Surely seems good to sleep in a bed again for a change. It's the first time in nearly five months.

I haven't had any letters for about two weeks but neither has anyone else in the outfit so I guess I can't complain.

By the way, I found Orville Spurgeon in the bed beside me. Sure seemed good to see him. He has a goatee about two inches long. I didn't know him at first. I guess he has the flu. He was trying to look me up but had never been able to get far enough forward to find me.

I'm sitting here in bed writing this. In pajamas too! First time I've had them on in a long time. In fact, it's the first time I've slept with my shoes off in ages.

Well, it looks like I'd soon have to close for this time.

Dear Folks, Love Orlie

Things are going pretty good over here – should soon be over with. Write when you can. I'll try to drop you a line again soon. Tell everyone "hello" for me.

Love,
Orlie

Orlie Meskimen

> May 13 - July 30, 1943 – The Regiment was engaged in police and salvage work, training and building staging areas for those troops bound for Sicily.

▼

Tunisia (postmarked New York)

May 13, 1943

Dear Folks,

Just a few lines to let you know I'm okay and thinking of you. I got about 10 letters from you a few days ago. They were postmarked from 8 April to about the 17th. All in all, I got about 20 letters that day. I'll surely be busy getting all of them answered. There were letters from you, LaVonne, Jack Graham and Richard Narber. Things are quiet once again so I'll be able to do quite a little writing during the evenings in the future.

I'd surely like to be home so I could help with the painting and shingling. I suppose it is nearly done by this time. It sure will make the old home look different. I suppose the lawn and the flowers are growing pretty fast these days.

I've had my first bath for about a month this last week. Even used a tub in some Frenchman's back yard. We were getting pretty rank – ha! But we're all cleaned up now and feeling perfectly swell.

I sent you a picture some time ago that was taken in one of these towns. There were three of us sitting at a table. The one on the right was, I believe, Sgt. Harvey McDougle, and

Dear Folks, Love Orlie

the one in the center is Corp. Dick Emery (John's brother). By the way, the Detachment has had several letters from him since he's been home.

Well, it looks as if I'd soon have to close for this time. I'll write more sometime soon. Write when you can. Tell everyone "Hello" for me and to write to me.

Love,
Orlie

Orlie Meskimen

▼

Tunisia (postmarked New York)

May 17, 1943

Dear Folks,

Today is Sunday and since I've a little time I'll write you a few lines. I'm feeling fine and in the best of spirits. I haven't heard from you for nearly a week, but there hasn't been very much mail. We should be getting some more within the next few days.

I ran into Dale Vogt the other day. It was the first time I'd seen him since the trip here. I've seen all the Shellsburg fellows with the exception of King in the past month. It just seems he and I are never near each other.

I suppose you have heard the good news by this time. We're all pretty proud of ourselves and glad it's over. I've collected a few little souvenirs which I hope to be able to bring home with me.

I burned the roof of my mouth this noon eating some very hot meat and vegetable hash. It's pretty sore. We're eating good now and getting back to normal a little. Surely seems good.

I rather imagine the old "Burg" looks a little bare with all those places of business gone. But I guess present day circumstances do make people head for the largest towns. Cedar Rapids must be a pretty busy place now.

Looks like I'll have to close for this time. I'll write again soon. Write when you can and take care of yourselves.

Love,
Orlie

Dear Folks, Love Orlie

------------ ▼ ------------

Tunisia (postmarked New York)

May 19, 1943

Dear Folks,

After reading an article in the current Stars and Stripes magazine I find it is permissible for you to send me packages weighing up to 5 lbs without a written order from my company commander. I would very much appreciate it if you would send me a box about once a week. I'd like to have candy and gum especially. You could also enclose other sweets and etc. It's been so long since we've had very much of that sort of thing. You can use the money from my savings account.

Things are going about the same as usual with me over here. We have authorization to tell quite a great deal about our experiences over here now so I'll be writing letters telling you about some of the things I've done and seen. There have been lots of incidents which I have had happen which I know I'll never be able to describe vividly enough to make anyone really understand just how I felt. I guess one just has to go through it to ever realize just what it's like.

Well, guess I'd better close for this time. I'll write more within the next few days. Tell everyone "Hello" for me and to write. I'll be able to write lots of letters in the future.

Love,
Orlie

Orlie Meskimen

▼

Tunisia (postmarked New York)

May 20, 1943

Dear Folks,

Received two letters from you yesterday. They were postmarked 21 and 22 of April. So it takes nearly a month for your letters to reach me. Most of them take less time than that though. Your V letters are being photographed now – are mine? For awhile I thought they were but I'm not so sure now.

Yes, I know the Gaddy boy and the other boy you wrote about. In fact, I was with them when the incident you spoke of happened.

I also got several letters from LaVonne and one from Jack Graham. Mail service hasn't been so bad. By the way, if you know Jo Popenhagens address please send it to me. I owe them a letter but I've lost their address so I can't write.

My face is all healed up now from the infection I had. It took a long time because sometimes I wasn't able to take care of it. It was an infection called "Infantigo" that spreads under the skin and is very difficult to heal unless dressed all the time.

I should be able to write lots of letters now. I'll try to write about twice a week. I've so many people I should write to. For a long time I wrote only to you and LaVonne, but I should be able to find time to write to everyone. Looks as though I'll have to close for this time. Write when you can.

Love, Orlie

Dear Folks, Love Orlie

▼

Tunisia (postmarked New York)

May 22, 1943

Dear Folks,

I'll endeavor to tell you about a little of my battle experience in this letter. I have been in 6 engagements – 3 of them major. There were 3 defensive and 3 offensive. First was a defensive battle at Kef-El-Amar Pass – then two defensive battles near Sbiba. Both times we repulsed the enemy with little difficulty.

Then comes the offensive. Once again at Kef-El-Amar Pass where those fellows you spoke of were captured (Private Kenneth Gaddy of Vinton was one). Then in a large scale attack where we had 96 artillery pieces firing one of the heaviest concentrations used in this war. Tanks attacked enemy machine gun and mortar positions time and time again. The final result being that the enemy was driven from Fandouk Pass and the nearby hills.

Then came the attack on Hill 609. One of the best attacks ever made with tanks and infantry combined. Lots of prisoners were taken. I lost 3 men throughout all these battles which really is pretty good considering that we were under heavy artillery and machine gun fire all the while.

The enemy is a clever and vicious fighter. He gives no quarter and asks for none. Most of them are young – barely out of their teens.

Well, I guess I'll have to close for this time. I'll write

again soon. Tell everyone "Hello" for me. Kelly and Urevig were two of the men I lost. I think I have pictures of them back there. Write.

Love,
Orlie

Dear Folks, Love Orlie

▼

Tunisia (postmarked New York)

May 26, 1943

Dear Folks,

This will be just a few short lines to let you know I'm okay and thinking of you. I've been doing lots of writing lately. I never had time to write for such a long time and now that I do have I write 2 or 3 letters every day. I've about caught up on my writing.

By the way, I'd like to have you send me a small, fairly cheap camera. You could also send me about 12 rolls of film. I could really get some nice pictures now. They would surely be nice after all this is over. I understand you can send me one 5 lb box per week now. I guess you have to show my letter asking for boxes to the postmaster. Send the camera as soon as you can. You can show this letter to Kathleen. Tell her I'll surely appreciate those boxes.

The Germans surely lost a lot of men and equipment down here. There are thousands of burned tanks, cars and trucks. Also huge ammunition, ration and gas dumps. For awhile there mostly all of us had a German car of some sort to drive. But, they took all of them away from us.

Well, it looks like I'll have to close for this time. I'll write more in the next few days. I've got to write to LaVonne yet tonight and its rapidly getting dark.

Love,
Orlie

Orlie Meskimen

▼

Tunisia (postmarked New York)

May 29, 1943

Dear Folks,

Here I am writing again today. It was just a few days ago that I wrote to you last. I received a letter from you today – also one from Clare. The one from you was written May 7, so that wasn't so bad. I believe the mail service is getting better all along now. It's been taking about a month for one of your letters to reach me.

The weather here has been splendid. The days cool and breezy and the nights just cool enough to sleep well. We've had bombing attacks nearly every night but nothing serious. Nothing at all compared to what we're sending back to them. All in all, we're really not doing so bad. Plenty of rest, food and a nice area.

I've had lots of letters from LaVonne lately. I believe she's set on hooking me for sure. She surely talks like it at any rate. She's a darned good kid – I think an awfully lot of her. Not the same feeling I had for Diane. Guess I really don't know just how I do feel. It's been a long time. All my ideas about everything have changed – for the better though, I believe.

Well, it looks as though I'll have to close for this time. I'll write again soon. Write when you can and tell everyone "Hello" for me.

Love,
Orlie

Dear Folks, Love Orlie

▼

Tunisia

May 31, 1943

Dear Folks,

Today is Memorial Day so I'll write you a few lines. We had a very nice service today for those who have been killed and those who will be. There were talks by both our Catholic and Protestant chaplains. There was a volley fired over a casket draped with our flag. It was really quite a nice service. It made me think that all the trouble we've had was really worth it. I don't believe I'd mind so much now if I had to lay down my own life. It was a glorious death and a glorious thing that they gave the supreme sacrifice. All in all, it was surely a nice service.

George King was over and spent the day with me. I surely had a good time talking over old times with him. He had his arm in a sling – nothing serious – just a little infection from a vaccination. Most of the old fellows who were in Claiborne with me are gone now. I've got a lot of Easterners. I still have Emery, Timmins, Gardner, Carlson, Osborne, Foster and Rhodes. Guess you have pictures of some of them.

I understand Diane is engaged to some fellow in Cedar Rapids. Surely hope she is happy. I realize now we could never have made a go of it. Especially now. I know I've changed since I've been over here. I haven't heard from her for nearly two months but in her last letter she mentioned this fellow. I've never met him but I guess he's okay. Diane deserves the best of everything – her father has always made life miserable for her.

Well, I guess I'd better close for this time. I'll write more soon. Write when you can.

Love,
Orlie

Dear Folks, Love Orlie

▼

Tunisia (postmarked New York)

June 2, 1943

Dear Folks,

Today is the second day of June and a very hot day indeed. I just came back from a dip in the Mediterranean. It's really swell – we have a nice beach and the water is perfect. I'm acquiring a nice tan all over. We swim naked and spend lots of time lying in the sand.

I got 3 letters from you today and 2 from LaVonne. A lot of our mail must get lost. It seems we don't get as much mail as we should.

It kind of tickles me to hear about Ted Emler being in the army. He always told me he'd get in before it was over. I always liked Ted – he was a darned nice fellow.

LaVonne B. seems very positive we're going to get married when we get home. I guess maybe it's a pretty good idea at that. I think quite a lot of her, perhaps I love her. It's been so long I really don't know. I guess she wouldn't make such a bad daughter-in-law at that, would she? Well, I guess I'd better close for this time. Write when you can.

Love,
Orlie

Orlie Meskimen

▼

Tunisia (postmarked New York)

June 8, 1943

Dear Folks,

Received a letter from you today. It was the one where you were worrying about my being in the hospital. I'm sorry I never told you in the letter I wrote from there. I should have told you what was the matter. I really think I had a little touch of malaria. I'm feeling swell though now – gaining back some of the weight I lost during the recent action.

It's nearly time for chow so I guess maybe I'll have to knock off. It's 5:15 and we eat at 5:30. We've been getting very good rations lately. Plenty of cakes for breakfast, good fresh meat and lots of dehydrated vegetables. Maybe I'll have time to finish before supper at that. Guess my wristwatch is a little fast. I've an issue watch. They are 17 jewel Elgins. Nearly all Sergeants are issued them. Mine was pretty accurate up until some of the shelling we went through. Since then it hasn't been so good – gains about 5 minutes in a days time.

Well, guess I'd better ring off. I hear the bugler blowing mess call. I've a terrible appetite lately; go back for seconds and sometimes thirds. I usually eat about 8 cakes in the morning in addition to eggs, cereal, bacon, bread and coffee. So you see I'm really not doing so bad.

Lots of love,
Orlie

Dear Folks, Love Orlie

---- ▼ ----

Tunisia

June 10, 1943

Dear Folks,

This will be just a few short lines to let you know I'm okay and thinking of you. I'm enclosing a picture of a "Jerry" soldier and a couple of German stamps. I'll send more of this stuff later.

The weather has been perfect here of late. The days breezy and the nights cool. We have a swell breeze coming off the sea nearly every day. I've never seen better nights for sleeping. I go to bed nearly every night about 9:00. We get up at 0500 so it means we have to go to bed early. We're surely living a healthy life. Plenty of good food, lots of sleep, and all the fresh air in the world.

I suppose the days there are getting hot now. The grain is all ripe here now. They have about the most crude means of thrashing I've every seen. Horses walk on the grain to shake the kernels out. The Arabs in this part of the country are very diligent workers in spite of the fact that they have very little machinery.

Well, guess I'd better close for this time. I'm sending this via air mail and I don't want it to be too heavy. Write when you can. They must be holding our mail up again because we're surely not getting any. Guess will probably be morning again.

Love,
Orlie

Orlie Meskimen

Tunisia

June 19, 1943

Dear Folks,

I've been getting a little mail again now. In the past week I've had letters from you, LaVonne and Tom. Surely seems nice to be getting a little mail again. Tom is feeling fine and having lots of fun. I wouldn't trade places with him though. Seems funny that I should go all through this action down here and never get a scratch and he nearly gets killed in an automobile accident. He's still got wire in his chest where the broken bones were.

I'm going to an open air movie tonight. It's "Casablanca". Should be a good show. They surely do everything they can to entertain us while we're not busy. The last show I saw was "Priorities on Parade" – it was a darned good show.

Send me a copy of the letter that was printed in the papers. I can't seem to think what I did write about. It was surely good to see Orville Spurgeon though. It was the first time I'd seen him since I was home at Christmas time nearly two years ago.

Well, guess I'd better close for this time. I'll write more again soon. Write when you can. Our mail will all catch up with us sometime. Tell everyone hello for me.

Love,
Orlie

Dear Folks, Love Orlie

▼

Tunisia

June 23, 1943

Dear Folks,

Here are a few pictures of Germans I'd like to have you save for me. I haven't time to write very much but I wanted to send them today. They are typical of Jerry.

Our mail service is getting better again these days. We get a little mail nearly every day now. I've had about 15 letters in the last 3 or 4 mail calls.

You can put these in my album if you like. Reserve several pages because I'll probably send more later. Write when you can. I'll write another larger letter soon. I'm feeling swell these days. Lots of sleep, good food and sunshine.

Love,
Orlie

Orlie Meskimen

▼

Tunisia

June 27, 1943

Dear Folks,

Received four letters from you yesterday and was so glad to hear from you. Our mail service is rapidly getting better now. All in all, I got 8 letters – really not bad!

The weather here has been pretty warm of late. The ocean breezes have died down a little. I've been having a little trouble with my feet due to the hot weather. Had slight touches of athlete's foot. I've been painting them with iodine and soaking them in some solution the medic's prescribed. Nearly everyone is having some trouble.

Marjorie Graham writes to me quite often these days. Don't know what ever possessed her to start writing. She writes a very nice letter. Very impersonal and conversational. She tells me that she wants to take up flying but says Russell wants her to continue school.

Well, it looks as though I'd soon have to close for this time. I may have a pleasant surprise for you one of these days. I'll tell you more about it later. Write when you can and I'll do the same.

Love,
Orlie

Dear Folks, Love Orlie

▼

Tunisia

June 28, 1943

Dear Grandmother,

Received your nice letter a few days ago and was so glad to hear from you. I've been getting lots of letters lately. Keeps me busy trying to answer all of them. It's sort of hard for me to write a decent letter now. There's so little news from here now. Now that all the action is over there's very little to write about.

I was awfully sorry to hear about Mary's little boy. But things like that just happen and even though it's tragic there's not a thing we can do about it. I've seen so much of it that it will take a long time to forget.

Things have been pretty uneventful the past month or so. I go to outdoor movies once or twice a week but outside of that there's very little to do.

We're eating very good now. Good food and lots of it. You see, we only recently became a company. We're no longer a detachment as you've probably noticed by my address. Not only do we rate more men but we have our own kitchen. Always before we were attached to some other outfit and that never worked out so well. I have radio and phone sections, intelligence section, message center section, ammunition to pioneer section, and a platoon of 37 MM anti-tank guns in my outfit. The sections operate for our battalion. It's really interesting and educational work. I have a splendid outfit – one of the best in the business.

Orlie Meskimen

Well, looks like I'll have to close for this time. Write again soon – I always enjoy your letters.

Lots of love,
Orlie
P.S. If you ever need any money for anything don't hesitate to use my savings!

Dear Folks, Love Orlie

Tunisia

June 29, 1943

Dear Folks,

Today is Sunday and a beautiful day. I just came back from church and it was so cool and nice sitting here in the shade that I thought it would be a good time to write a letter. We have a new chaplain and he's a pretty good speaker.

There are a few things I'd like to have you send me. First there's cigarettes – we aren't getting many through our canteen now so I could use about two cartons a month – Lucky's – a carton every two weeks. Then, I could use some Vasoline hair oil. My hair is getting pretty dry and I want to take care of it. Another thing I really appreciate would be about five pounds of fudge. I've been awfully hungry for it the past few days. I guess you will have to show this to Kathleen in order to send me this stuff.

News is awfully scarce over here now. Everything is quite calm now. There was quite a storm for awhile though. Kelly is back now none the worst for the wear. He was hit in the hip but not very serious.

Write when you can. Your letters are coming through good again. You'll have to excuse my writing. I've got a small book I'm writing on. Tell everyone "hello". Tell Kathleen if she passes these packages I might take her to dinner and the theater when I get home.

Love,
Orlie

Orlie Meskimen

Tunisia, North Africa

July 2, 1943

Dear Folks,

Well, it will soon be July 4th and it promises to be hot here. The past few days have been very hot indeed. Even the fore part of the nights have been warm. Makes our wool blankets rather uncomfortable to sleep between.

I'm enclosing a theater ticket from Tunisia. I'd like to keep it for a souvenir – also the menu for our Christmas dinner last year which was of course on the boat enroute down here.

I'm going to see a French girl show tonight – should be pretty good. Some of these French and Italian girls are pretty nice. Naturally it's hard for us to get next to them because we don't speak their language.

We're finally wearing cottons. We wore wools until about a week ago. They were beginning to get pretty uncomfortable. It's hotter here now than it ever gets in Iowa. It's going to be good for me though. I'm entirely over the old trouble I used to have with the heat.

Well, I'm going down and take a shower before supper. We've improvised a shower from a steel drum, cans and a water pump "Jerry" left behind. I'll finish this after supper.

Here I am back again. I just received a commencement exercise announcement from Marjorie Graham. Send her $5 from my savings as a little gift.

Well, guess I'd better close for this time. Write when you can.

Love, Orlie

Dear Folks, Love Orlie

▼

Tunisia, North Africa

July 7, 1943

Dear Folks,

Well, July 4th has passed again. I went to a baseball game in Tunis in the afternoon. It was a game between my regiment and another from my division. We got beat but it was a good game. It was the first I'd seen since I left the states. I'm thinking maybe I'll play a little myself later on. If you will remember I hurt my arm pitching in school. The weather is hot here and I think perhaps I can heal the old trouble.

I saw a pretty good show last night – "For Me and My Gal". It was a story of World War I. We're getting lots of entertainment along that line now.

I suppose Tom is pretty anxious to hear from me. I wrote him several letters last month. Also one so far this month. So he should begin to hear from me soon.

I was surely surprised to hear about young Ferguson and Strawhacker. They seem like little boys to me. This is a pretty tough game – bigger, older and stronger fellows than them couldn't stand the gaff. But I guess with ample time and adequate training they will be as good as any. Perhaps it will never be necessary to use them. Surely hope not.

Well, it looks as though I'd soon have to close for this time. Your letters are coming through nicely now. Write when you can.

Love,
Orlie

Orlie Meskimen

▼

Tunisia, North Africa

July 11, 1943

Dear Folks,

Received a letter from you today and was so glad to hear from you. It was written June 25 so that really isn't so bad. The package you sent should reach me before so very long. I hear from LaVonne quite regularly too.

I suppose you've heard the latest news by this time. Surely hope this venture is successful – it will mean a lot to all of us. I really believe it will come out okay. Of course, there's so little I can say but I'm sure you know what I'm talking about. It is pretty exciting though.

Our canteen supplies are coming through better now so you won't need to send me as many cigarettes as I originally asked for. Send me about three cartons and then stop until I ask for more.

I just finished a complete physical examination – lungs, heart, eyes, teeth, ears, throat, hernia, etc. Marked excellent so I guess I'm in pretty good shape.

I've been doing quite a little reading of late. The Red Cross gives us reading materials – Readers Digests, those pocket size books and etc. Then of course, we get the Stars and Stripes. I never send them home anymore because there is only a limited number so we must pass them around.

Well, guess I'd better close for this time. I'll write again soon. I'm going down and listen to the news and find out how the boys are doing in Sicily.

Love, Orlie

Dear Folks, Love Orlie

Tunisia, North Africa

July 15, 1943

Dear Folks,

Today I've been overseas 18 months. Surely seems like a long time. The day I landed in Ireland seems like 5 years ago. But perhaps by this time next year I will be home again.

I'd appreciate it if you would send a set or two of amber colored sun glasses in one of the boxes you send me. The sun is getting very intense – it's causing me to squint too much. They don't have to be anything very expensive. Be sure they have pretty long bows and are pretty wide across the face piece.

I was rather surprised to hear about the Maxson's having another baby. I got a letter from them today. Besse wrote it from the hospital – said they named him "Jimmy".

Tell Edna Bergen for me that I said for her not to worry. It won't do any good and Bob surely wouldn't want it. I imagine it is pretty tough for her but she can rest assured that it's twice as tough for Bob.

Well, it looks like I have to close for this time. Write when you can. Tell everyone "Hello" for me.

Love,
Orlie

Orlie Meskimen

Tunisia, North Africa

July 21, 1943

Dear Folks,

In the past week I've received about 10 letters from you. I've received several letters from you in which you said you had sent me boxes but as yet I've never gotten them. I guess they probably travel a little slower than the letters though. I'll probably get them in the next week or so.

Everything is burned to a crisp here now. The old olive trees are about the only thing that's green and even they don't look very good. It surely gets hot and dusty during the days.

I saw the Life magazine with the pictures and article about Hill 609. I've been over that ground where those two pictures were taken. Those pictures were taken from pretty well down the hill. Just behind where the cameraman was standing the hill rises very sharply. He was standing just in front of the main German positions. The picture of the wrecked Jerry tanks was taken along the road to Mattus. We were on our way to Hill 609 when we passed them. They were knocked out by British dive bombers. Write when you can.

Love,
Orlie

Dear Folks, Love Orlie

▼

Tunisia, North Africa

July 22, 1943

Dear Folks,

    This will be just a few short lines to let you know I'm okay and thinking of you. I didn't know I had to write a letter for every box you send me. In the future I'll try to write about one letter a week requesting boxes. Never send me any hard candy in the boxes because we're tired of it. We get some through our kitchen ration. Send me candy, gum, and cigarettes in the next box. Take the cigarettes out of the carton and they will pack better. I haven't received either of the boxes you've sent but they should be getting here soon.

    Things are going pretty good in Sicily now, aren't they? Shouldn't be long before it falls. Maybe it won't be so long before the whole thing will be over.

    I got a letter from some Lint who works with dad at the lumber yard. I couldn't read the return address. Let me know who it was so I can answer the letter. Write when you can.

Love,
Orlie

Orlie Meskimen

▼

Tunisia, North Africa

July 25, 1943

Dear Folks,

    This will be just a few short lines to let you know that I'm okay and thinking of you. I haven't had any mail from you for about a week now but I'll be getting some soon one of these days. Our mail service has been pretty good recently though. Last week I got about ten letters so that really wasn't so bad.

    I saw a double feature at our open air theater last night. It was "Tarzan in New York" and "Pride of the Yankees". I didn't like the first one so very well but the last one was really swell. It was surely a fine tribute to a truly great athlete. Gary Cooper should be very proud of his portrayal of Lou Gehrig. It was surely pathetic the way his baseball career had to end.

    The weather doesn't seem to cool off very much around here. For the past two months the weather has been sticky and humid during the days. It rained a little last night just before dark but not enough to help that much. It was even hotter after the rain was over with. The ground is so dry that the water soaks much faster than it can fall. When we first landed down here last winter it rained darn near all the time. I suppose it will start to rain again this fall sometime.

    Well, it looks as though I'd soon have to close for this time. I'll write more again soon. It's awfully hard for me to think of very much to write about

Dear Folks, Love Orlie

anymore. Nothing exciting ever happens so there really isn't very much to write about. Write when you can and tell everyone hello for me. I owe so many people letters now that I'm a disgrace but I just can't seem to get in the mood to write very much. Maybe I'll get in some more excitement one of these days and I'll have something to write about again. Tell the Mason boys hello for me and that I said for them to write. They're awfully close to me. Maybe it's because they seem to enjoy the same things as I do.

Love,
Orlie

> Aug. 1, 1943 – The Regiment moved to Arzew near Oran for more training and a week later to the vicinity of Slissen for mountain training and the 5th Army Battle School.

Tunisia, North Africa

August 8, 1943

Dear Folks,

Received ten letters from you today and also the first box. Was certainly glad to hear from you and to get the box. Everything in the box was in perfect order. I will surely enjoy the gum. That's one thing that we very rarely get anymore. Those were the first American candy bars I'd had for about three or four months. You can send another box of about the same kind. If you haven't already sent the sun glasses I sent for please send them in this next box. My eyes bother me quite a lot in this African sun. The light is so intense that it makes me squint a lot. Any cheap pair will be okay. It might be a good idea to send a couple of pairs in case I lose or break the one pair.

I also got letters from LaVonne, Clare and Richard Narber. Richard writes to me pretty often these days. He's finished elementary flight training now and is being sent to another field for either fighter or dive bomber instruction. He always did like the air corp.

I had to take this letter out of the machine for a couple of hours because I had a few reports that had to be finished tonight. I have them all made

Dear Folks, Love Orlie

out now so I'll finish this letter. I had to make them out in quintuplicate so it was quite a job.

I suppose everything is going about the same there in Shellsburg these days. I was surely surprised to hear about Jay Moody. I guess he was in pretty bad shape though. He never took care of himself so I guess he's paying the penalty now. Working on the railroad is too hard a job for a man who refused to take care of himself.

It looks like I'd soon have to close for this time. I'll write more within the next few days. Write to me when you find time. Tell everyone hello for me and that I'm in the best of spirits and feeling swell. I'll write to Clare again one of these days. Tell Linder that what he told Verna Dickson worked out just about that way.

Love, Orlie

Orlie Meskimen

▼

Tunisia, North Africa

August 11, 1943

Dear Folks,

This will be just a few short lines to let you know I'm okay and thinking of you. Of course I haven't been writing very much lately. I really don't know why. I guess it's just because I can't think of very much to say. I got the second box you sent yesterday. Everything was in excellent condition and the candy was perfectly swell. You can send me another as soon as you get this letter. I'd like to have another of about the same contents as the last one.

It's now 7:30 in the morning and it's pretty cool. The nights are awfully cool and damp. Our clothes have a damp, sticky feeling in the morning. The days are usually pretty hot though. It's beginning to look a little like fall now. Of course most plants haven't been green for a long time but those that are, are starting to turn a little brown now. It's hard to realize that it's August already. This summer has certainly flown by.

I've been seeing quite a number of movies lately. Last night I saw a British film called "In Which we Serve". It wasn't a bad show if you like British movies. They're so different than ours that sometimes they're hard to understand. Their sense of humor is vastly different than ours. The American boys seldom laugh at what the British boys think is extremely funny. I've got a lot of respect for the British who fought here in Africa. They're excellent soldiers.

Well, it looks as though I'd soon have to close for this time. I'll write again soon. Drop me a line when you find time. Your mail to me is coming through in good time now. I've had letters from you as late as July 24. Tell everyone "hello" for me and those who care to write to write also. The news sounds pretty good these days doesn't it? Maybe this thing will be over with before anyone realizes it.

Love,

Orlie

Orlie Meskimen

▼

Tunisia, North Africa

August 17, 1943

Dear Folks,

    I haven't had any letters from you for about a week but should be hearing from you again soon. The mail service has been pretty slow these past two weeks. Maybe it will pick up soon though. I got a nice letter from Jo Popenhagen with a picture of their little girl enclosed. She surely is growing up. I was surprised at how much she had changed since the last picture they sent me. I guess all the kids around will be grown up so much that I won't know them by the time I get home again. Some of the boys who are getting into the services now were just kids when I saw them last.

    We have a very nice entertainment schedule arranged for this coming week. There is some form of entertainment every night. There's a movie every night and a double feature some nights. Most of the shows that are coming are comparatively new. Tonight we have the show "China Girl" plus some coffee and doughnuts that will be served by the Red Cross before the show. All in all, we're having a good time, good food and plenty of good sleep. Everyone is getting in the pink of condition. We were all pretty well run down right after the battles were over. In battle situations it is often difficult to get food and water to the men, but all that is over now and we're getting along fine. One of my very good friends was killed today and I feel pretty rough about it. He used to be one of my staff sergeants. I've probably mentioned the name to you in some of my letters. His name was John Currie. He was promoted to 2nd Lieutenant just a few days ago and now this had to happen.

Well, it looks like I'd soon have to close for this time. I'll write more again in a few days. Write when you can. Tell Linder to write me another letter when he finds time. Tell everyone I said "hello". I also got another letter from Marjorie Graham. She writes awfully nice letters. From her letters I get the idea that she's dating a little. Seems like no time since she was a little girl.

Love,

Orlie

Orlie Meskimen

Tunisia, North Africa

August 20, 1943

Dear Folks,

Received six letters from you yesterday. As a general rule that's the way they actually come – quite a few at once. You mentioned in several of them that you had sent the box of fudge. I haven't received it yet but the packages are usually slower than letters. It will probably reach me in the next week or so. I'd surely appreciate it if you would send me another of the same. Chocolate candy is one thing we never get through our canteen ration.

I've been seeing some pretty good shows recently. We're having one every night now. Tonight I'm going to see "Palm Beach Story" – it should be pretty good.

I've been having a bad toothache the past couple of days. I'm going to have it pulled this morning. That will be five teeth. I'm going to get a partial plate. All of these teeth were well back in my mouth so they don't show, but the plate will help me chew.

Well, it looks as though I'd have to close at this time. I'll write again soon. Your mail is getting here in about 15 days now and that really isn't bad. Write when you can. I got a letter from Earl Mason yesterday too.

Love,
Orlie

Dear Folks, Love Orlie

▼

Tunisia, North Africa

August 21, 1943

Dear Folks,

    I'm writing you a few lines to let you know I want my address changed. Using the other one sometimes delays our mail because it goes to Regimental Headquarters company. I've just switched it around a little.

    Today's mail isn't in so I don't know if I will hear from you today or not. I should be getting the last box you sent. Perhaps it will get here today. I'll surely be glad to get my glasses. I really need them down here.

    I'm sending you some souvenir handkerchiefs from Ireland. I had them packed away and just found them today. Hope you enjoy them. They are hand made from pure Irish linen. I sent LaVonne a set of them too.

    I was surprised to hear about Jay Moody dropping dead. I guess he was in pretty poor physical condition though. He always drank too much liquor. Well, guess I'll have to close for this time. I've got to attend a meeting of all 1st Sergeants at regiment at 7:00. It's now 6:15 and I just finished breakfast. Write.

Love,
Orlie

Orlie Meskimen

▼

Tunisia, North Africa

August 25, 1943

Dear Folks,

    This will be just a few short lines to let you know I'm okay and thinking of you. I haven't heard from you for about a week but we haven't been getting very much mail so I guess that accounts for the delay. I got a nice letter from Wilma Narber yesterday. She seems to be very happy with her married life. Says that LaVonne and I will have to come and visit them when I get home again. I got three letters from LaVonne about a week ago but none since then. Her mail from the west coast comes very irregularly. When it does come there is a lot of it. I haven't as yet received the box of candy you sent but it should be coming along one of these days.

    The days are hot and the flies very pesky over here now. I never saw too many flies or any that were as persistent as these in Africa. We take the best control measures we know but they still seem to hang around. Our kitchens are all fly proof so they don't get at our food anymore than we can possibly help.

    It's hard for me to realize that it will soon be the first of September. If I were home now I'd be starting to get my guns in shape for the season's hunting. I'll bet Linder is getting all excited now getting ready to open the squirrel season down by the dump bridge. He and I were always the first to get in there in the fall. He is a very good shot.

Dear Folks, Love Orlie

One of the best I ever saw. He would make a great sniper in the Army. I used to like to hunt with him better than anyone else I know. He was a comical guy to be around.

Well, it looks like I'd soon have to close. I'll soon have this blank full. Write when you can and tell everyone hello for me. I try to answer all the mail I get but sometimes I lose the letters before I get them answered so I don't write. Always try to keep my letters until I get them answered.

Love,
Orlie

Orlie Meskimen

> Aug. 26, 1943 – The Regiment moved to Bou Tlelis where training was eased up and passes to Oran were available.

▼

Tunisia, North Africa

September 2, 1943

Dear Folks,

Received two letters from you and one from LaVonne. Surely glad to hear from you. LaVonne seemed to think I was mad at her. I can't figure out what made her think so but I guess it will be okay anyway. I wrote jokingly and told her I wasn't going to write until I heard from her again. I've had about ten letters from her this past week so I guess she must have believed me.

It hardly seems to me that it's the first of September. This past year has gone so fast. Doesn't seem like any time since I was in Ireland. The weather here now is getting a little like fall – the nights are exceedingly cool and damp.

I checked up on the amount I have in soldier's savings and it's nearly $600. It draws 4% interest which is the best I know of. I only put $20 in this month because I was a little short – trips to town on pass are pretty costly. But I guess a fellow's got to have a little fun once in awhile.

I know the outfit Bob Bergen is in. I was pretty near him once. Wish I would have known he was here. I'll drop him a line as soon as I finish this. I'd surely like to see him. Guess I'll have to close for this time. Write when you can.

Love, Orlie

Dear Folks, Love Orlie

Tunisia, North Africa

September 3, 1943

Dear Folks,

Received a box today. It was the one that had all the candy bars. They are certainly good. Thanks a million! The next thing I'd like to have you send is a good heavy wool sweater. It should be the pullover type with long sleeves. I'd like it to be brown. The size is 38 long. Even if I stay here this winter I will need it. The nights are getting awfully cool already.

Our mail seems to be coming pretty slow now. It goes by spells – sometimes it comes along good and other times not so good. We'll possibly be getting a lot one of these days.

I have a little radio in my tent now. It surely seems good to hear some music. I like "As Time Goes By", "There Are Such Things" and "Knock Me a Kiss". We have a station here called the AEF program. It's pretty good. I understand they plan to send it by short wave to the states so perhaps you will be hearing it.

Well, looks like I'd soon have to close for this time. I'll drop Kathleen a letter one of these days and thank her for the cigarettes. Write when you can. I'll write again one of these days.

Love,
Orlie

Orlie Meskimen

▼

Tunisia, North Africa

September 6, 1943

Dear Folks,

This will be just a few short lines to let you know I'm thinking of you. I'm enclosing a couple of pictures – one of myself and one of Currie – the fellow I told you that got killed in an accident. It was about the biggest blow I've ever had. We were buddies since Camp Dix in New Jersey. He was one of the cleanest, nicest guys I've ever known. The other picture is of me doing a little typing in an olive grove we were in. These two pictures should give you an idea of the intense light down here during the days.

I wrote a letter to Bob Bergen yesterday. No doubt I'll be with him one of these days or at least near him. Things are definitely looking better all the time. Shouldn't be much more than next spring for "Fritz" – next fall for the Japs. The tables have finally turned and it's just a matter of time now.

I got a letter from you today but haven't received any more boxes. They should be coming through pretty soon though.

Well, folks, I'll write again soon. Write soon. Tell everyone "hello".

Love,
Orlie

Dear Folks, Love Orlie

Tunisia, North Africa

September 8, 1943

Dear Folks,

Just a few lines to let you know I'm okay and that I got a couple of letters from you yesterday. So glad to hear from you. They were dated 15th and 20th of August which really isn't so bad. I also got a letter from LaVonne and one from the Masons. I got Kathleen's letters the 6th and will answer it soon. I'd already written her one letter.

I've received only one of the boxes so far but they will all come through. I'm still eating candy bars from the last one. They were surely good. The pecan rolls came through in good shape. Any bar with nuts on the outside do. Those with chocolate covering are inclined to stick to the wrapper and cause a little trouble. I'll drop Clyde a line and thank him for the cigarettes. It was awfully thoughtful of him. Seems like Oscar's kids are awfully close to me.

Well, it looks as though I'd have to close for this time. I'll write again soon. Drop me a line when you find time. Dale Gillis certainly has gone to town. I believe I can do more good where I'm at.

Love,
Orlie

Orlie Meskimen

> Sept. 9, 1943 – The 100th Infantry Bn. was assigned as the Regiment's 2nd Bn. and fought as part of the Regiment until March 1944.

▼

Tunisia, North Africa

September 9, 1943

Dear Folks,

    I'm writing this letter in order to send you a picture of me that was taken about a week ago. I'm thinner than I've been in some time but I guess there are reasons for that. I'm rather out of uniform too. I have on a wool shirt and denim battle trousers. They are the new type with the large pockets similar to the British battle dress. Hope you enjoy this picture. I'm sending one to LaVonne too.

    The weather is getting like fall here too. The days are still pretty hot but the nights are very cool and damp. We turned in all our cottons for wools the other day. The wools are a little warm during the days but comfortable at night. I policed up a canvass Army cot about two months ago so I haven't been sleeping on the ground lately. It's the only time since I've been in Africa that I've slept in a bed except for a few days in the hospital that time.

    Dale Vogt, Homer Woodson and Orville Spurgeon have been over to visit me several times lately. Also I see George King nearly every day. All of us are pretty close together now. They all look good especially Homer – he's very tan and exceptionally healthy looking. The Army has been very good for him. He's surely a changed man these days.

Dear Folks, Love Orlie

I suppose you heard the news about Italy last night. All of the fellows are surely tickled. It will help us to bring Germany to her knees just that much sooner. By next spring the European campaign should be over and the Japs by next fall. There's not a doubt in my mind but that I'll be home by this time next year at the very latest.

I've had a radio around for the past week or so. Some of the songs I like are "Taking a Chance on Love", "Brazil", "I've Heard That Song Before", "There Are Such Things" and "It's Murder He Says". Are they still pretty popular over there? We had Al Jolson in person at our open air theater a few weeks ago – he puts on a pretty good show.

Well folks, guess I'd better close for this time. Write when you can. By the way, what's Mrs. Dickinson's address. I'd like to write her a letter soon. Thank her for the gum and explain to her that I'd have written sooner but I didn't know her first name. She's a grand old lady – I always thought a lot of her and admired her flowers immensely.

Love,
Orlie

Orlie Meskimen

▼

Tunisia, North Africa

September 12, 1943

Dear Folks,

 I thought I'd drop you a few lines today because I have a couple of things I want to enclose for souvenirs. Keep them for me because they will be nice to have later on. The picture is of some South African French Colonial troops. They were our allies in the recent Tunisian campaign. Very good allies to have as you will no doubt notice from their picture. They are every bit as tough as they look too. These fellows are guarding some Italian prisoners. The tower near them is a guard's lookout tower. The French bill is now no good except for a souvenir. All the money down here is very much alike in appearance. We've been using the following: Bank of Morocco, Bank of Algeria and Bank of Tunisia. Last month, however, we were paid in American currency. It was the first time since we left the States. It surely seemed funny but mighty good too.

 I saw a very good show last night. It was "Stage Door Canteen." It had the biggest all star cast of any picture ever made. I laughed so much I thought I'd die at some of the characters. Tonight I'm going to see "Rebecca." I don't know what kind of a show it is but I've heard it's pretty good. We've been having some pretty good shows lately.

 I see George King nearly every day now. He comes over to my company for dinner quite often. We've got one of the best kitchens in the business

Dear Folks, Love Orlie

so maybe that's the reason. We've been getting a lot of fresh beef these days so we're pretty well fed.

No doubt there will be a break in my letters again soon. It rather looks as though I'd be pretty busy again soon. Don't worry though because I've got a feeling that everything will be okay. Just keep writing and before you know it this thing will be over and I'll be writing to you again.

I told you some time ago that I thought I'd have some good news for you in the near future. At the time I was angling for a promotion to Lieutenant. Since then I've thought it all out and I believe I can do more good where I'm at. It would mean getting separated from the boys I know and have been with a long time. If I were in the States it would be a different thing. As a Lieutenant I wouldn't make as much money as I do now. You see they have to pay for their meals so I really wouldn't be as well off.

I haven't received anymore boxes but then our mail hasn't been coming through very good. Maybe the service will pick up again at least when we get where we're going. I'll surely be glad to start getting mail again. Occasionally they let a V-letter through but not very often.

I don't have Tom's address so I can't write to him. He never writes anymore so I don't know where to write to. I'd surely appreciate it if you would send me his address so I could write to him. All the fellows are interested in what he's doing and would enjoy writing to him too. He probably thinks I don't want to write and I surely don't want him to think that.

Orlie Meskimen

Well, folks, I'd better close for this time. Write soon and tell everyone hello for me.
Love,
Orlie

Dear Folks, Love Orlie

▼

Tunisia, North Africa

September 16, 1943

Dear Folks,

I received a letter from you today and the box with the candy and sun glasses yesterday. I was so glad to hear from you. I also got letters from Marjorie, LaVonne and Jack Graham. Marjorie writes to me quite often these days. Say's she plans to attend university this fall although she wants to be a pilot. I guess Russell must have laid down the law to her.

It is awfully rainy this past week. It's the first rain we've had in months. At first it was pretty welcome but it's getting a little tiresome now. The dust doesn't bother us now so that's our consolation. It was so terribly dusty before the rains began.

Yesterday I finished 20 months overseas. In some ways it doesn't seem that long and in other ways it seems much longer.

There really isn't much I'd like you to send me for Christmas. Just send me the candy and nuts and I'd like the sweater I asked for some time ago. The weather here now is pretty cool at night and it would sure be nice. Well, guess I'll have to close for this time. Write when you can and keep smiling.

Love,
Orlie

Sept. 19, 1943 – The Regiment sailed from Oran in readiness for an assault landing in Italy.

Orlie is listed as participating in the following engagements in Tunisia, North Africa:

- Hadjeb El Aioun, February 17, 1943
- Sbiba, February 19-21, 1943
- Kef El Almar Pass, March 10, 1943
- Fondouk Pass, April 8-10, 1943
- Hill 609, April 29-30, 1943
- Edde Khila, May 4-7, 1943

SEPTEMBER 1943 ITALY

Sept. 22, 1943 – The Regiment landed in the Bay of Salerno without incident and marched to the Division assembly area near Paestum.

Sept. 26 - Oct. 2, 1943 -- The Combat Team advanced in the general direction of Benevento against moderate to heavy opposition.

Oct. 3, 1943 – The 3rd Bn. made a spectacular advance and secured Benevento advancing through difficult terrain, drizzling rain and heavy artillery fire. Company "K" suffered heavy casualties in the outskirts of Benevento. In the afternoon the 45th Infantry Division passed through.

Oct. 5, 1943 – The Regiment assembled Northwest of San Giorgio.

Orlie Meskimen

Italy

October 8, 1943

Dear Folks,

    Sorry I didn't write sooner but circumstances just didn't permit.

    I had the biggest thrill of my life a few days ago – I met Bob Bergen. If there were ever two guys who enjoyed seeing each other it was us. My morale went up about 1000%. I happened to run across his outfit. That should also enlighten you. We surely talked over old times. He said he couldn't see where I'd changed one bit, and he looked just the same to me. He certainly is proud of his wife and baby. I wasn't with him 5 minutes until he dragged his pictures out. We gave the Reynolds girls hell in general too. I was the first home town fellow he'd met since coming overseas.

    I suppose it's beginning to look like winter around the old burg these days. I always used to enjoy the fall in Iowa. It always meant the hunting season wasn't far away. Well, it looks like I'll have to close for this time. Hope you can read this. Write when you can.

Love,
Orlie

Dear Folks, Love Orlie

Italy

October 10, 1943

Dear Folks,

Received a letter from you today and was so glad to hear from you. So far I have received four of the seven boxes you sent me. Parcels aren't coming through now so perhaps that explains why I'm not getting them. No doubt I'll get them sooner or later. I'll surely appreciate the sweater – it's starting to get rainy and cold now. It will surely be a good thing this winter. I really think I'll be home by spring, not discharged but at least in the States. Maybe it will be before then.

I got a letter from LaVonne with four pictures and a letter from the Pogles in yesterday's mail too. Dorothy says that they are expecting another baby soon – guess they really plan to raise a family. It sure as hell isn't going to take me long either. This war business takes all the devilty out of a fellow and makes him ready to settle down.

Well folks, it looks like I'll soon have to close for this time. I'll write more again in the next few days. There may be times when I won't be writing again but don't worry.

Love,
Orlie

Orlie Meskimen

> Oct. 12, 1943 – The Regiment moved to a bivouac area West of Mountsaichio assembling as Division reserve during the crossing of the Volturno River.

▼

Italy

October 13, 1943

Dear Folks,

 I received 4 letters from you today. I also got letters from LaVonne, Kathleen Nettell and Clare. I was surely glad to get so much mail. Parcels still aren't coming through so I guess I'll have to wait for them. I was glad to hear you got the sweater and sent it on to me. The weather is pretty cold and rainy these days.

 I haven't seen Bob Bergen since that one time but we should be running into each other occasionally. It surely was a treat to see him again. It was worth $100 to see him.

 I'm feeling swell these days. Eating lots and, in general, in the best of condition. Must be the change in climate. I weigh about the same as always. I was pretty slim when that picture was taken of me typing. That was just after the Tunisian campaign.

 Well, folks, guess I'll have to close for this time. Keep writing and I'll write as often as I can. Tell everyone hello. Tell Clyde I said he'd better watch those women.

Love,
Orlie

Oct. 18, 1943 – The regiment was given the mission of crossing the Volturno river and securing Alife. The 1st Bn. secured a bridgehead, and the following day Alife, with the 3rd and 100th Bns. securing the flanks.

With all of the regiments across, the Red Bull men fought their way through grape arbors and villages until they reached the third crossing sites. On October 21, 1943 Col. Ray Fountain, Des Moines, Iowa, received orders rotating him to the States and Lt. Col. Carley Marshall was placed in command of Iowa's 133rd Infantry Regiment.

By the time the 34th Division units reached the third Volturno crossing sites, they had yet to dry out their clothes and boots from the first two crossings. However, they had gained considerable experience in crossing rivers.

Oct. 23, 1943 – The Regiment advanced against stiff opposition to secure finally the high ground Northwest of San Angelo D'Alife. During that day the 100th Bn. beat off a tank attack, accounting for one enemy tank.

Orlie Meskimen

▼

Italy

October 27, 1943

Dear Folks,

Just a few lines to let you know I'm okay and thinking of you. Sorry I haven't been writing oftener but circumstances just don't permit. Maybe at a later date I'll have some time and will be able to write more often. Don't worry, however, because I'll write whenever I get a chance.

I've been getting lots of letters this past week. I've had letters from you, LaVonne, Russell G. and Tom Pick. I haven't had Tom's address so I couldn't write to him.

I'm going to make some coffee as soon as I finish this letter. I carry a little field stove with me that's about the best thing the Army ever came out with. I surely like my coffee.

I haven't shaved for nearly a week so I'm pretty whiskery. Maybe I'll get to my razor again one of these days so I'll be able to get cleaned up.

Well, folks, looks like I'd have to close for this time. Write when you can. I'll write again as soon as I can. Tell everyone hello for me.

Love,
Orlie

Dear Folks, Love Orlie

Oct. 31, 1943 – The Regiment captured Ciorlano which required capturing a succession of hills and supplying by hand carry.

Nov. 4, 1943 – The third crossing of the Volturno was accomplished and S. Maria Olivetto taken against heavy enemy fire and over ground thick with mines and booby traps.

Nov. 5 - 9, 1943 – The Regiment repelled numerous enemy counter-attacks and by the 12th was relieved by the 135th and 179th Infantry Regiments.

---------▼---------

Italy

November 11, 1943

Dear Folks,

This is the first letter I've written you in quite some time. Sorry I haven't been able to write more often but existing circumstances just don't permit. Maybe we'll get a break one of these days and I'll be able to catch up on my letter writing.

I've been getting quite a few letters in the past few weeks. I've heard from you, Mason's, LaVonne, Marjorie and several others. I also got one of the boxes about two weeks ago. It was the one that had the gum from Mrs. Dickinson in it. Thank her for me. I'll write her a few lines some day when I have more time.

I've never seen Bob again but he's very near – it's just

that we can't go see each other. I read the 91st psalm and I think I agree with Bob. Someone or something has surely been with me this past month. I'll tell you all about it later on when censorship permits.

It's beginning to get real cold over here now. I'll surely be glad to get the sweater you sent. The weather corresponds pretty much with that in Iowa.

Well, folks, looks like I'll have to close. Write when you can. May God bless all of you.

Love, Orlie

Dear Folks, Love Orlie

▼

Somewhere in Italy

November 16, 1943

Dear Folks,

I received the box with the sweater in it today and you have no idea how glad I was to get it. The sweater surely feels good – I put it on as soon as I got it. It was exactly what I wanted. The handkerchiefs were very nice and something I needed too. Of course the candy is always welcome. The day is cold and rainy so you can imagine how much I appreciate it. We are getting a few days rest so I have my tent set up. It's about the size of the one we used to have for camping. I have it all alone so I have plenty of room for my field desk, equipment and a place to sleep. In combat all this luxury stays behind and I have exactly what I can carry on my back. We were on the line about 28 days so you can see we really needed rest. It's awfully good to have a place to sleep outside of a trench and hot meals. In combat we get either "C" or "K" rations. The "C" consists of six cans – 1 can hash, 1 meat and beans, 1 vegetable stew and 3 cans of biscuits. There is also coffee for one meal, cocoa for one and lemonade for the other. The "K" isn't nearly as good. Well, folks, it looks like I'd have to close for this time. I'll try to write again tomorrow. Write when you can.

Love,
Orlie

Orlie Meskimen

> Nov. 15 - 22, 1943 – The Regiment was in VI Corps reserve.

Somewhere in Italy

November 18, 1943

Dear Folks,

    Just a few lines to let you know I'm okay and thinking of you. The sun is shining today for the first time in about a week. It surely feels good – brings everybody's morale up 100%. The mail hasn't come in yet today so I don't know whether I'll have any or not.

    I'd like you to send LaVonne $25 again this year for Christmas. There's nothing I can send her from over here. She will be able to get something she wants that way too. She's certainly a fine girl and I still think a lot of her after being away nearly two years. I'll soon be overseas two years – January 14th. In some ways it doesn't seem that long and in some ways it seems much longer. But it won't be long now. I feel sure you will see me before school is out next spring. There is a lot of talk about relieving some of the old men who have been overseas a long time. It surely seems no more than fair. But I guess the best thing is to wait and see what happens. Well, it looks like I'd have to close for this time. I'll write soon again. Write when you can and tell everyone hello for me.

Love,
Orlie

Dear Folks, Love Orlie

> Nov. 25, 1943 – The Regiment relieved the 504th Para. Infantry in the vicinity of Colli, while the Cannon Company moved to Scapoli.

▼

Somewhere in Italy

November 27, 1943

Dear Folks,

Just a few lines to let you know I'm okay and thinking of you. I've had several letters from you but have been busy and so wasn't able to answer until now.

I was awfully sorry to hear you had been sick, Grandma. I surely hope you are better now. They always say you can't keep a good Irishman down, so I don't worry much about you. Take care of yourself though – you've worked too hard too long. If you need a girl around the house go ahead and hire one and I'll pay for her.

I just got back from a few days vacation in Naples. Had a very good time. The rest was of course plenty welcome too. Generally speaking, Italy is much the same as Africa but I believe the towns are a little better here – especially the large cities. I wanted awfully to visit the Isle of Capri during my stay but couldn't make the right connections. Perhaps I will still have an opportunity to go there.

I was glad to hear Uncle John was better. He's getting pretty well along in years and he's worked awfully hard too, so maybe it's more or less to be expected. You folks should try to influence Sam to move him to town where he can have better care.

Orlie Meskimen

I bought two little souvenirs while I was in Naples. I bought a mother of pearl rosary for LaVonne and a sea shell with some very nice hand engraving on it. It has a landscape scene with Mt. Vesuvius on it. Mt. Vesuvius is a volcano here in Italy you know. It's really quite quaint and unique.

I've never seen Bob since that one time. I rather doubt if I will see him soon because we're rather far apart now. Perhaps some time in the future I'll run across him again.

Well, folks, I'm running out of anything to say. By the way, I had a very nice Thanksgiving dinner – turkey, dressing, potatoes, celery, olives, bread, butter, jam, coffee and Jell-O. Write when you can. May God bless all of you.

Love,
Orlie

Dear Folks, Love Orlie

▼

Somewhere in Italy

November 28, 1943

Dear Folks,

Just a few lines to let you know I'm okay and thinking of you. I got one letter from you today and was so glad to hear from you. It was the one in which you mentioned the two tubes of Vasoline hair oil. Send them along with some candy. I'll be very glad to get it. I'm letting my hair grow out again. It was only about 1-1/2 inches long. It's beginning to get cold now so I think longer hair will be more desirable.

In your letter you also spoke about LaVonne B. being sort of mad at Diane. She wrote me a letter saying she was planning on marrying me regardless of what I thought about it. She's an awfully nice girl and the fact that she's Catholic doesn't mean a thing to me. We threshed all that out long ago and thoroughly understand each other. Too many people are finicky about religion these days. I have my own religion and no one will ever change my ideas. I've seen too much in the past year not to believe. No matter whether a person is a sinner or the best Christian, when God figures our time on earth is up it's all over. I've seen both fall over here. I'm fully convinced that something more than my own battle prowess has been with me – I've had too many narrow scrapes for it to have been coincidence. Write when you can. God bless all of you.

Love,
Orlie

Nov. 29, 1943 – The Regiment continued the attack against bitter opposition for the next 5 days with the enemy always looking down from the next hill. Casualties were as high as 15% in the 100th Bn. The weather was cold and rainy and all supply was brought up by newly acquired mules.

Before the 34th Infantry Division stood the snow-capped mountain peaks of Monte Pantano and Monte Marrone, where the Germans had anchored in what they felt would be their winter line. The crisp air of early winter was bone-chilling. In the valleys below the formidable mountains stood the Red Bull men in sleet, melting snow and a quagmire of mud, wearing wet uniforms and shoes. Throughout the area men could be seen attempting to help tanks, artillery, and trucks out of hub-deep mud. To make matters worse, the Dogfaces had not yet been issued winter uniforms.

On November 29, 1943, Col. Frederick Butler's 168th Infantry, on the left, set out to take Monte Pantano. On the right flank, the 133rd Infantry, commanded by Col. Carley Marshall, moved out to attack Monte Marrone, remembered by veterans as Sawtooth Mountain.

Monte Pantano will be recalled by participants on both sides as a short-lived brutal battle. Men of the 133rd Infantry have no fonder memories of Monte Marrone, although the Germans did not defend Old Sawtooth with quite as much courageous vigor.

Success at Pantano first appeared imminent as the 168th cleared out foothill blockhouses, but in a saddle near the crest the Germans counterattacked like demons possessed. Capt. Benjamin Butler (no relation to Col. Butler) led Company A, 168th Infantry in a brutal bayonet attack time after time to drive the enemy from their lines. The 168th Infantry troops met the enemy eyeball to eyeball midfield with assault fire, then drove them back with bayonet and rifle butts. All day and all night the battle raged.

Running low on ammunition, some of the 168th Infantry men threw C ration cans at the charging enemy who, in the darkness, mistook them for grenades, thus buying enough time for those with a few rounds to reload and fire. Grimly the 168th Infantry held on, advancing inch by inch, refusing to give up ground gained.

On the right flank the 133rd Infantry and attached 100th Battalion relieved the 504th Parachute Infantry and pushed forward in a series of attacks to better anchor the lines, thus preventing the flanking of their positions and those of the 168th Infantry. After heavy fighting, they seized the left slopes of Monte Marrone and outposted Cerasuola.

The Germans pounded both Pantano and Marrone viciously with mortar and artillery fire, then strafed the area with fighter planes. Still the 168th and 133rd Infantries refused to budge.

It was at this point that a fortuitous development occurred. Sgt. Norman Raner, Company I, 133rd Infantry, now of Perry, Iowa, discovered an abandoned radio, somehow left behind when an Allied forward observer was wounded or killed. Testing it, he found an American artillery outfit on the other end. He could see enemy artillery firing on Pantano and directed highly effective fire on their positions. Raner later was given a battlefield commission and assigned as an observer with Cannon Company, 133rd Infantry.

On the night of December 3, the 135th Infantry Regiment relieved the 168th Infantry. Attacks and counterattacks continued on both sides, and casualties climbed. At last, on the night of December 8, the 34th Division was relieved by the 2nd Moroccan Division.

Brig. Gen. (Ret.) Ed Bird, then Lt. Col., 168th Infantry, can raise his right hand, minus two fingers, and attest to the ferociousness of the battles. All three of the regiment's battalion commanders--Bird, Albia, Iowa; Lt. Col. Floyd Sparks, Centerville, Iowa; and Lt. Col. Wendell Langdon--became casualties.

Coming down out of the snow-covered mountains, above the tree lines, was a terrible experience for the men of the Red Bull. They were totally exhausted, and some had trench foot so bad that they could hardly walk. Litter bearers operated in relays, only carrying casualties in excess of five miles. Some casualties slid down the hillside, while others had to be lowered by ropes down steep cliffs.

Dear Folks, Love Orlie

▼

Somewhere in Italy

December 1, 1943

Dear Folks,

Just a few lines to let you know I'm okay and thinking of you. I got two letters from you yesterday. They were both old letters – written in September. I can't understand why they were so long reaching me. I've received letters from you written in November already.

It's hard for me to believe it will soon be Christmas. Time surely flies over here. I guess it's because we're so busy. It will soon be two years since I've been home. I feel confident that it won't be so much longer. Things look pretty good on all fronts now. It's a slow process here because of the mountains. It's a matter of driving them off one hill after another. We take a hill and "Jerry" is on the next hill waiting for us to attack again – which we always do.

I've received letters recently from Merle Keiden, La-Vonne, Kathleen, Maxson's, Marjorie and Linder. I try to answer all of them but there are many times when I can't write. Even now there is mortar and artillery fire falling sometimes within a few hundred yards but it's all in a day's work. Write when you can and God bless you.

Love,
Orlie

Orlie Meskimen

Dec. 3 - 10, 1943 – The Regiment held positions won and was constantly subjected to heavy artillery fire.

▼

December 3, 1943

Dear Folks,

This will be just a few short lines to let you know I'm okay and thinking of you. I haven't heard from you for about a week but there haven't been many letters coming through so perhaps that explains why I haven't been getting many letters this past week or so. No doubt the letters will be coming in again soon though. There is an awfully large amount of Christmas boxes coming in now and there probably will be for the next few months. Last year we got packages all the way from early November until about the last of March.

All of us are feeling pretty good these days except for a few colds. I've had a nasty chest cold for the past three days. Nothing very serious but just enough to make me miserable at night. I guess I caught it sleeping on the ground with just my overcoat on. It's awfully hard to carry very much into combat so we don't have very much in the line of sleeping equipment. At the present time I have my headquarters in an abandoned Italian house so it isn't bad. Everything is pretty tough now. "Jerry" is getting more stubborn every time we make contact but we're not letting it bother us very much. It's going to be a long, cold winter here especially with "Jerry" getting reinforcements all the time. We used to out number him pretty decisively but I think we're about even up now. These Germans are young and very determined. They are true Nazi's. They fight viciously and seldom give up until they are faced with certain wounds or death. These American kids are learning to play for keeps too.

Well, folks, write when you can and I'll try to write as often as possible. Tell everyone hello for me. I guess this will have to be all so wish everyone a Merry Christmas and a Happy New Year for me. Tell some of the people to write because I'm always glad to get mail.

Love,

Orlie

Orlie Meskimen

▼

Somewhere in Italy

December 6, 1943

Dear Dad,

    Received your letter yesterday and was so glad to hear from you. The mail service as far as letters goes hasn't been very good this past two weeks. They are trying to get as many boxes through as possible. But the letters will start coming through again one of these days.

    That was a pretty big order you gave me in your letter but I'll do the best I can. I've gotten a few so far but they're getting harder to get all the time. Everyone counts though.

    The fighting is getting tougher all the time. Jerry is really making a fight for it now. He's pretty stubborn but in spite of his stubbornness we're rapidly making him give ground. I wouldn't take a million dollars for my battalion – I fully believe they're the best in the business. They simply can't be beaten. There aren't many of us old fellows left but the new men are all fighters. There are only six of the original boys from my company left. Myself, Timmins, Dick Emery, Gardner, Foster and Traber. Well, dad, looks like I'd have to close. Write again when you find time. Tell everyone hello for me too.

Love,
Orlie

Dear Folks, Love Orlie

> Dec. 9, 1943 – The Regiment was relieved by the French.
>
> Dec. 10, 1943 – The Regiment moved to the vicinity of Alife to a rest area where replacements were received and a program of training and recreation was provided.

▼

Somewhere in Italy

December 13, 1943

Dear Folks,

Just a few lines to let you know I'm okay and thinking of you. I finally got your other Christmas box and everything was delicious. The candy was the best I've had overseas and it was really fresh. I'll drop Clare and Mrs. Fish a letter of thanks. Clare's gift was very nice and something very handy. I'd like to send him a picture of myself but I don't have any and can't get them.

I got a very nice letter from LaVonne a few days ago. She has everything planned for our future. She says she thinks we should be married about a month after I get home. Looks like I'm really caught this time. No doubt but that she'll get her way. I like her an awfully lot – far more than I ever cared for Reynolds. But I guess all this talk doesn't interest you.

This pen drops ink all the time – guess I'll have to buy a new one. Well, folks, guess I'll have to close for this time. Write when you can. I'll try to write again in the next few days. Tell all the folks hello.

Love, Orlie

Orlie Meskimen

▼

Somewhere in Italy

December 18, 1943

Dear Folks,

    Just a few lines to let you know I'm okay and thinking of you. I got one letter from you today. It was the first I'd had for quite some time. You said you hadn't been hearing from me very much lately. It's because I was on the front for 28 consecutive days. It was really a grind too. I sometimes thought my number was up but somehow I managed to pull through. But it's all in a days work so I guess I can't complain very much.

    I'm getting letters from LaVonne real often these days. Guess she figures I'm not such a bad guy after all. Said she figured I was pretty fast when she first dated me – I didn't waste any time. After figuring it all out I guess maybe she'll be Mrs. Doug Meskimen. She seems to think it would be a pretty good deal too.

    They may not photograph this because the form is pretty badly beaten up. Write when you can. I'll try to write a letter every day now. Tell everyone hello for me.

Love,
Orlie

Dear Folks, Love Orlie

▼

Somewhere in Italy

December 19, 1943

Dear Folks,

Today has been a cloudy, miserable day. It threatened rain all day but never seemed to get around to it. It's clear tonight so perhaps tomorrow will be a nice day. The past week or so has been swell in the days, sunny and warm – feels like spring in Iowa.

Did I tell you I got a letter from Nellie Riffee and also one from Anne Wiggins? Anne wanted to know if I was a stamp collector. Said she would send me some of her collection if I was. I could collect all kinds of stamps over here if I wanted them. All in all, both letters were very interesting. I've answered both of them already.

I suppose you folks are getting ready for Christmas by this time. I guess I'll be off the front then. We've been off about a week now and hope to stay off until after the first of the year. We've been having passes and movies nearly every night so our morale is considerably better than about three weeks ago. Write when you can. I'll write as often as I can. God bless all of you.

Love,
Orlie

Orlie Meskimen

▼

Somewhere in Italy

December 23, 1943

Dear Folks,

    Just a few short lines to let you know I'm thinking of you. It will soon be Christmas day and I surely wish I could be with you. It's been rainy and cold all day here so it doesn't seem very much like Christmas. The mud is terrible too. But I guess I shouldn't complain because it looks like I'll spend Christmas day off the front. I'll probably be back in combat by New Year's Day or shortly thereafter. Things are going pretty good here now – looks like we'll take Rome sometime in March. By then there should be plenty popping everywhere. The invasion of the continent should be well on its way by that time.

    LaVonne writes pretty often these days. I usually get three or four letters each week. I also get some nice Christmas cards – from Clarence's, Clare, Maxson's, you folks, LaVonne B, Diane, and many others. I don't have cards to send back but I guess they will understand.

    I'm sending a little box of souvenir coins, currency and etc. There is also a sea shell with an engraving of Mt. Vesuvius. It is one of the oldest and biggest volcanic mountains in the world.

    Well, folks, guess I'd better close for this time. I'll write again soon. There will probably be a break in my letters soon again. But don't worry, "Jerry" hasn't got the best of me yet and I don't intend to let him now. It's too late in the game.

Love, Orlie

Dear Folks, Love Orlie

▼

Somewhere in Italy

December 27, 1943

Dear Folks,

    Just a few lines to let you know I'm okay, in the best of spirits and hoping your holiday season is a happy one. I had a very good dinner and we had lots of entertainment during the day so we had a pretty happy Christmas.

    I cabled $400 to you for my savings. Surely hope you get it okay. I won the money shooting dice. How much do I have with it? My company clerk tells me I have $982 in soldier's savings now. It draws 4% interest so it isn't a bad deal. I usually put in from $35 to $50 each month. Sometimes more if the dice are good to me.

    I'm enclosing a couple of souvenirs. One is written by my regiment commander, Carley L. Marshall. He's a great leader, one of the best in the business. As you probably know, those Hawaiian born Japanese make our other battalion. We only have two white battalions in my regiment. These Japs are good Americans and excellent combat soldiers. Well, folks, guess I'll have to close.

Love,
Orlie

Orlie Meskimen

▼

Italy, of course

December 28, 1943

Dear Folks,

I'm sending you a picture of Castlenouva – a small Italian village. We fought hand to hand battles with Jerry here and also drove him from the hills in the background. He put up a hell of a fight here but with no avail.

Christmas is over and we had a pretty good time considering everything. We had a very good dinner, church services, movies and some good music.

It's acting very much like snow here tonight. The wind is rising and it's getting pretty cool. In a way, I'll be kind of glad to see some good snow again.

Well, folks, I've got some work to do so guess I'll have to close. Take awfully good care of this picture. It has some pretty unpleasant memories but I still want it. Write.

Love,
Orlie

Jan. 1 - 5, 1944 – The Regiment was in II Corps reserve.

Jan. 8 - 13, 1944 – The Regiment was teamed up with the 1st Special Service Force under Task Force B and continued the attack, seizing several hills, including Mt. Capraro, in the face of stubborn enemy resistance, mountainous terrain and adverse weather.

Jan. 13, 1944 – The Regiment less the 100th Bn. reverted to control of the 34th Infantry Division and continued the attack Northwest of Cevaro. The 100th Bn. returned to the Regiment on the 19th of Jan.

Orlie Meskimen

▼

Italy, of course

January 19, 1944

Dear Folks,

    This will be just a few short lines to let you know I'm okay and thinking of you. Sorry I haven't been writing oftener but I guess you know the circumstances. There really isn't much I can write about because I haven't been doing very much lately outside of fighting and you've probably been reading all about that.

    I got quite a surprise today. It was a Christmas card from the Reynolds family. At the end they had written, "You're doing a grand job and we're proud of you." I was really surprised to get it.

    Well, folks, guess I'll have to close for this time. I probably won't be writing very much. Drop LaVonne a line because I won't have time. Tell her I love her and that I'll write as soon as possible. Well, I've got to go.

Love,
Orlie

Jan. 21, 1944 – The Regiment occupied positions in preparation for the attack across the Rapido river to Cassino. Cassino was extremely well fortified, the enemy skillfully employing the terrain features to best advantage.

Jan 24 - Feb. 21, 1944 – The Battle for Cassino. The Regiment played a leading role in this famous battle which was one of the toughest of the war. There were many cases of outstanding valor and the fierceness of the battle can be gauged by the over 50% casualties suffered by the three Battalions.

To the Red Bull foot soldiers it appeared that Italy was made up of mountains, villages and Volturno Rivers. They had fought three vicious series of battles and crossed the Volturno three times. Wet and miserable, the valiant troops continued the crossings, driving back enemy defenders, only to repeat the action all over again. Minefields, machine guns, mortars, multi-barreled rockets, and enemy artillery fire continued to cut sharply into the ranks of the 34th Division. The Red Bull men literally bartered their arms, legs and blood for each objective.

Crossing the Volturno became a nightmare for the Red Bull Dogfaces. After each crossing they looked hopefully to the rear, expecting to see a fresh unit coming forward to relieve them and give them an opportunity to dry out or change their wet clothing. This proved to be wishful thinking, for relief never came. On and on they fought, clearing the enemy from such towns as Limatola, Amorosi, Ruviano, Caiazzo, Margherita, San Angelo, Alife, St. Angel de Alife, St. Leonard, Castello de Alife, Dragoni, Pratilia, Para, Santa Maria Olivetto, Roccaravindola, Ravindola, Montaquila, and Fillignano. To those who didn't speak Italian, the names of towns on the maps looked like an Italian restaurant menu. Strengths dwindled more with each engagement. Replacements received were few, and--without rest--weariness was overtaking the men, but move on they did.

Heroes were so numerous during the Volturno battles that it would not be possible to do them justice in this article.

Wet, worn and weary, the Red Bull warriors at last were given a short respite in squad tents erected amid the smaller mud puddles near St. Angelo de Alife. Time was spent cleaning clothing and equipment, bathing at portable shower units, and training hundreds of badly needed replacements. Oh yes--they enjoyed an occasional beer and rest on a cot! The Red Bull men hadn't even partaken of Christmas dinner before the 135th Division was alerted to go back up front. The 36th Infantry Division, after its most creditable performance of the war, had seized San Pietro, but had bogged down before reaching San Vittore.

In succeeding days the 34th Division regiments relieved their 36th Division counterparts, and the Red Bull battlers went about the gruesome task of driving Germans out of the Italian mountains.

After house-to-house fighting, the 135th Infantry drove the Germans from San Vittore. The terrain became rougher and rougher in the 10-mile stretch from Lenoci to Radicosa. There were no vehicular roads, only a few footpaths, and above the tree lines even these were obliterated in a glaze of snow and ice.

Movement of supplies and evacuation of wounded became a horrendous task. Pack boards were strapped to men's backs and mules were pressed into service to carry much needed ammunition to isolated locations. Casualties in some instances were carried up to 14 miles on litters. The 109th Medical Battalion finally had to be augmented with litter bearers from the regiment's support companies and extra details from line companies.

Day and night the raging mountaintop battles continued. Cicereli and surrounding hills were cleared. Only the looming Mount Porchio, Cervaro and Trocchio and their foothills stood in the division's pathway.

The 168th Infantry seized Cervaro. The 133rd Infantry combined with the elite 1st Special Service Forces (forerunners of today's Green Berets) to push the Germans from Mt. Majo, Mt. Vischataro and numerous hills in that area. Meanwhile, the 135th Infantry fought every step of the way up the approaches to Mt. Trocchio. All regiments fought brilliantly and in the end all of the hill masses were taken.

Adequate descriptions of these brutal

battles and of the adverse conditions under which they were fought is not possible in these writings. Those who fought through those miserable days and nights have them etched, like a horrible nightmare, in their minds forever.

With these strategic hill masses seized, the Red Bull men could, in the distance, see the Rapido River and the awesome mountains surrounding Cassino, where hundred and hundreds of them would become wounded or lose their lives.

Cassino and its surrounding hills, Belvedere Hills, Abate Hills and snow-capped Monte Cairo, presented a bone-chilling bulwark of defendable terrain and the Germans knew how to use it to greatest advantage. Cassino Abbey stood as a pillar of rock in the mountain's crags. This constituted the formidable Gustav Line, which was to become a thorn in the side of Allied Armies.

Across the Rapido, waiting to greet the Red Bull Division, was the 211th Grenadier Regiment of the 71st Grenadier Division, which held the town of Cassino; the 44th Austrians controlled the Massif. To the north, defending Mone Castellone and Monte Cairo, was the 5th Gebergestruppen (mountain) Division. Providing additional fire support was the 7th Werfer Regiment with six batteries of 150mm guns and two batteries of 210mm nebelwerfer rockets.

The 34th Division troops cleared the Rapido River banks, established positions, then prepared to launch a diversionary attack and render support fire for the 36th Infantry Division, assigned to make the initial crossing.

Minnesota's 135th Infantry faked a strong attack across the Rapido on January 10, 1944 as the 36th Division launched its crossing. Using minefields and withering machine gun, mortar and artillery fire, the Germans literally decimated the Texas Division, driving them back across the river, shattering their effectiveness as a division.

The 34th started probing patrols at once in an attempt to find a suitable crossing site. On January 24 the 100th Battalion (Hawaiian) crossed, but was driven back. Attempts at establishing a bridgehead were made by the 1st and 3rd Battalions, 133rd Infantry, but they were repelled with heavy casualties and the 3rd Battalion made still another unsuccessful attempt. The 100th Battalion succeeded, then--lacking armored support--again was driven back. Attempt after attempt to cross was made by the regiments, but to no avail.

On January 27, 1944 the 168th launched a ferocious river crossing attempt. Tanks bogged down and the infantry forged ahead in minefields. Under withering fire, without tank support, the 168th men had to move back. Further attempts by the 168th failed to establish and hold a bridgehead, as tanks were either mired in the mud or were knocked out.

Lt. Col. Harry W. Sweeting, the commander

of the 756th Tank Battalion then moved his unit upstream and, under cover of smoke, managed to get 23 tanks across the river. The 2nd Battalion, 168th Infantry, encouraged by tank support, then stormed across the river, drove the enemy back and surprisingly held its ground. On February 1, 1944 the 135th Infantry crossed the 168th bridgehead and took up positions. That same day the 133rd Infantry crossed and cleared out an Italian barracks area.

With the 168th Infantry holding ground in the vicinity of Caira, the 133rd Infantry moved toward the town of Cassino. The 135th Infantry moved up the hillside toward the Abbey. The 133rd Infantry reached the city of Cassino, fought a pitched battle, but succeeded only in taking and holding little more than half the town.

The 135th Infantry doggedly moved forward under the Germans' noses for days, fighting desperately to reach the Abbey, but had to be satisfied to reach it with patrols. Meanwhile, the 168th Infantry, in the higher elevations, made attempt after attempt, but was never able to drive the enemy from the hills. Col. Robert Ward, 135th Infantry Regiment Commander, became a casualty at Caira and Lt. Col. Charles B. Everest, Council Bluffs, Iowa assumed command.

Cassino was no doubt one of--if not the most--bitter large-scale battles fought during World War II. Neither side would yield. Unable to dig into the mountainside, men piled rocks around themselves for protection. But when mortar and artillery descended on them, the rocks shattered, creating even more shrapnel.

Feet froze, and men ran out of rations and ammunition because resupply could be accomplished only at night. In some instances men in isolated locations scavenged the dead for ammunition and rations. Still they held their ground. Strengths of units dwindled, as they fought off enemy counterattack after enemy counterattack.

Permission finally was granted to bomb the Abbey, which many felt was being used as an enemy observation post. (135th Infantry men who reached the wall said they had seen the enemy at that location.) On February 15, 1944 wave after wave of Allied bombers reduced the Abbey to rubble.

Gen. Alexander, Commander of the Allied Forces in Italy, who had learned of the 34th Division's depleted, exhausted condition from a member of his staff, finally ordered the 34th Division to be relieved by the British 4th Indian Division and the 6th New Zealand Brigade.

The 3rd Battalion, 133rd Infantry had succeeded in cracking the Gustav Line at one point, but were so low in strength that a deep penetration was not possible. Two men from Company L, under the command of Lt. Dennis F. Neal, Villisca, Iowa--Pfc. Leo J. "Pop" Powers, Anselmo, Neb., and Lt. Paul F. Riordan, Charles City, Iowa--both won Congressional Medals of Honor while cracking the vaunted Gustav Line.

Riordan was killed in action while leading his men in the capture of the jailhouse in Cassino. Had fresh troops been available to exploit the Gustav Line breakthrough, the battle for Cassino possibly could have ended sooner.

Down from the blood-spattered hills and out of Cassino came the brave Red Bull men, many with trench foot so severe that they dared not take off their shoes for fear that their feet would swell and they couldn't get them back on if the enemy attacked. Many had to wait for stretchers while buddies helped some down the hills. The feet of hundreds had to be amputated.

Companies were so badly depleted of manpower that it was not uncommon to find rifle companies, which were authorized 193 officers and enlisted men, down to 50 men and--in a few instances--30 men in strength.

The performance of the 34th Division at Cassino is etched deeply in the annals of military history. Despite the tendency of British historians to downgrade American military action while enhancing their own, British historian Dominick Graham, author of Cassino, had this to say about the Red Bull Division: "Considering the conditions and the unsuitability of some of their equipment, the performance of the U.S. 34th Infantry Division, a National Guard outfit, in coming within an ace of cracking the mountain defenses of Cassino, is almost beyond praise."

Graham goes on to quote Fred Majdalany, a British Indian Division company commander:

"The performance of the 34th Division at Cassino must rank with the finest feats of arms carried out by any soldier during the War. When at last relieved by the 4th Indian Division, fifty of those few who had held on to the last were too numbed with cold exhaustion to move. They could still man their positions, but they could not move out of them unaided. They were carried out on stretchers."

Only a small number of the heroes were decorated for their valor. In some instances those who witnessed the heroism were killed before the deed could be reported. Then too, the 34th Division was never known for handing out medals with the C rations. Besides, it would have kept the entire regimental staffs busy for a year writing up citations.

Cassino, in future years, became somewhat of a yardstick by which to measure the ferociousness of battles. Months later it would be learned that it took nearly five divisions of troops to shatter the bulwark at Cassino and accomplish what the Red Bull men came "within an ace" of doing.

Orlie Meskimen

▼

Somewhere in Italy

January 31, 1944

Dear Folks,

    Sorry I haven't been writing oftener but I guess you know the circumstances. Your mail has been coming through pretty good. I get letters from you usually about 2 or 3 days a week. I haven't as yet received the package with the hair oil but it should be coming through pretty soon.

    I surely was glad to hear how much money I had at home. It will come in very handy when I get home. I have nearly $1,000 in soldier's savings which will be given to me when I'm discharged. LaVonne has some money saved too. I don't know just how much but it will all help.

    I'm enclosing a few pictures as souvenirs. One is of a couple of Italian girls I know. The one on the right I dated a few times. She speaks English fluently and is bound and determined she's going to marry some Yank! She had designs on me but I guess she finally understands I'm not available. Her name is Wanda Comella and she has a fiery temper. Her mother is on the balcony above. She reminds me an awfully lot of Belle Greenwood.

    As you probably know I'm a year older now. I really don't feel a bit different than I did when I left home. Bob Bergen says he doesn't see a bit of change in me. I've never seen him since the one time. He surely looked good to me though. He looked just the same as he used to when he used to come to pick me up. Bob has a nice job. He's a radio technician in a regimental headquarters company.

Dear Folks, Love Orlie

His unit stays well in the rear. About all he has to worry about is bombs. Right now there are Jerry's within about 1,000 yards of me. I just had to take time to write a letter though. The artillery noise here is terrific and rather distracting. Most of it is outgoing though so we know Jerry is hugging Mother Earth and perhaps praying just a little. The dirty devils should each collect about five pieces of red hot shrapnel. Don't mind me – sometimes I guess I get so mad I can't think straight.

The boys are having quite a time kidding me about a little deal the other night. It seems I was grinding my teeth and one of the fellows asked me to stop. Still asleep, I said "I'm not grinding my teeth, I'm grinding coffee beans." When asked where I got them I said, "I carry them in my watch pocket." They've been kidding me ever since.

There are only six of us old fellows left. So you see I have almost a new company. By the way, Dick Emery is missing in action. I think he must have been hurt and captured after.

Well, folks, guess I'll have to close for this time. Write often and send me another box of candy and try to get me some Vasoline hair oil in Cedar Rapids. Tell everyone hello and give my regards to all.

Love,
Orlie

Orlie Meskimen

▼

Somewhere in Italy

February 6, 1944

Dear Folks,

Sorry I haven't been doing better at this letter writing but I've been so busy I can hardly find time to do anything for myself. Your letters have been coming through in good shape, though I haven't gotten the package yet but it should be here any day now. You can send me another package of candy – that's one thing we get very little of over here so it's truly appreciated. We're eating pretty good in spite of combat conditions. Of course, we get plenty of cold rations but there's always coffee so we don't fair so badly.

I don't think I told you before but Dick Emery isn't with me anymore. All the other old men are though. I was awfully sorry about Dick – he was one of my very best men. I should write a letter to John but I don't know his address anymore. Dick was awfully close to me – he sort of took Bob's place. I guess no one will ever take Bob's place entirely – we call each other "Brother" in our letters. We're already making plans for the future. Bob says I've got to get married as soon as I get home so we will be on an even footing again. He's a great guy, one of the best ever. I'd surely like to see him again but I guess that will be impossible for awhile.

Well, guess I'll have to close for this time. Write when you can. May God bless all of you.

Love, Orlie

Dear Folks, Love Orlie

▼

Somewhere in Italy

February 7, 1944

Dear Folks,

Here I am again with very little news but thought I'd drop you a line anyway. I've had a great deal of mail lately – don't know when I'll get around to answering all of it. I've had letters from you, LaVonne, Kathleen, Maxson's, Jean Evans and Bob. Bob writes real often. Of course, it only takes his letters about two days to reach me. It's awfully nice to have someone so close to correspond with. His letters always get to me even when the mail from the States is held up.

I just finished a letter to LaVonne and there are several more I should write but my hands are so cold it makes it hard to write decently. So I guess I'll wait until I can get in some place where my hands will be warm. The weather here now isn't especially cold but it's pretty crisp. It's beginning to look like spring now. They say the summer's here are nice but, of course, I don't intend to be here this summer.

Well, folks, guess I'll have to close for this time. Write when you can. Tell everyone hello.

Love,
Orlie

Orlie Meskimen

▼

Somewhere in Italy

February 12, 1944

Dear Folks,

Just a few lines to let you know I'm okay and thinking of you. Sorry I haven't been writing oftener but I guess you know the circumstances. It still will be a matter of a week or so before I can start writing in earnest again. Even now there are shells falling close. This battle is the toughest I've ever seen but we're gradually driving Jerry away from Cassino. In another week or so we should be getting a rest again. We surely need one badly.

The weather here today is beautiful – a lot like April in Iowa. There is snow on all the mountains around us but here in the valley the weather is swell.

The mail has been coming through darned good lately. I've had letters from you, LaVonne, Junior Reynolds, Delbert White and Marjorie during the past week. Delbert White just decided he should write me. I've got so many letters to write when we get back that it will keep me busy for a week at least. Then too, I've got quite a good deal of paper work to do. It's awfully hard to keep up with the paper work up here because of the moves and also because of enemy artillery.

Well, folks, looks like I'd have to close for this time. I'll write again as soon as I find time. Tell everyone hello for me. Maybe I'll be seeing you before so awfully long.

Love, Orlie

Dear Folks, Love Orlie

▼

Somewhere in Italy

February 16, 1944

Dear Folks,

Just a few quick lines to let you know I'm still okay and thinking of you. Sorry I can't write oftener, but I guess you understand the circumstances. It will probably be a week or so yet before I'll be able to write many letters. I'm writing this during a lull in activities. No telling when I'll have to stop. This thing should be over soon and I'll be able to write a letter every day.

The weather here has been pretty good. It's rather cool but the sun's out most of the time. All in all it's really not bad though. It will soon be spring here in Italy. There's lots of snow on the surrounding mountains but none here in the valley. Something tells me I'll be seeing you soon – all indications point that way. It's been a long time and I surely need a long rest. A fellow begins to feel as though his luck's running out.

Well, folks, guess I'll have to close for this time. Maybe by the time I write again I'll be off the front. I surely hope so. Tell everyone "hello" for me. Write when you can. I'll try to write again sometime this week.

Love,
Orlie

Feb. 22, 1944 – The Regiment was relieved and withdrew to Alife area for training.

Orlie Meskimen

▼

Somewhere in Italy

February 24, 1944

Dear Folks,

    I'm off the Front! After about 45 days I'm surely glad for the rest. I lost a lot of weight this time because of the constant strain. There were periods of a few days at a time when we were in reserve but we were always subject to German artillery fire and bombing. My company is wrecked beyond repair. Dick Emery is gone – probably captured. Joe Timmins is my supply sergeant so he never goes forward. I lost a lot of men. I had so many close calls myself that I'm pretty shaky yet. A fellow's nerves get pretty ragged after a few weeks.

    I got the box with the candy and hair cream – surely glad to get it. The candy tasted swell. You can send me some more of the same – including the hair cream. I'd like very much to get some Vasoline hair oil. I think you could have someone get it in Cedar Rapids. I'm letting my hair grow out again so I'll need plenty of that stuff to get it trained again. I'm planning very strong on being in the States before long so I want to look my best – LaVonne might not marry me if I look like the tramp I do now. In her last letter she said she'd marry me no matter what happened. She wants to get married shortly after I get home. I plan to take a few months off to write a book on some of my past experiences. It will be a nice souvenir. I plan to have it printed too. I've kept a pretty complete diary of each day's events.

    It's raining here tonight but I'm very comfortable in a

Dear Folks, Love Orlie

nice tent with my desk and a swell fire. There are 3 other fellows living here with me. It's swell not to have to sweat this out in a fox hole. It's terrible to have to live outside during a storm and with Jerry shelling in the bargain.

I'm more or less scribbling this letter. I'm laying on my cot trying to write this. I guess you'll be able to read it though.

George King was over to see me today. I'll be close to him as long as we're in this area. He only lives about 300 yards from here. Guess he came over to congratulate me on making it through another siege without getting hit.

Our battalion lost more than 75% of its strength in killed, wounded and captured at Cassino. The old 34th will never be the same again. If they don't do something for the original boys pretty soon there won't be any left. I don't think there are over 100 left in the whole battalion and there used to be well over 1,300.

I got a nice letter from Tom several days ago. I'll have to write to him tonight. I'm also getting letters steadily from a girl in Louisiana that I went around a little with after Diane sent my ring back. She says she never fully realized what a nice guy I was then. She's going to Iowa this spring and she may stop to see you. She has some pretty good pictures of her and I taken at the beach that she will show you. Her name is Ruby Aguillard – she's from Eunice, Louisiana. She's an awfully nice kid. There's really nothing between us but there probably would have been if I'd have been there longer.

Well, folks, guess I'll close for this time. Write when you can. Tell everyone "hello".

Love, Orlie

Orlie Meskimen

Somewhere in Italy

February 27, 1944

Dear Folks,

    Today is Sunday and a gloomy day. The sky is dark and threatening rain almost at any moment. We have had considerable rain this past week. Perhaps it will clear up soon though. I believe spring will come pretty early here. It isn't too cold now – seems like Iowa in early April.

    My mail is coming through very good now. I get several letters each time the mail comes in. The mail isn't here yet so I don't know how I'll fair today.

    It's about dinner time now so right after I finish this letter I'll be going to chow. Don't know what we're having but our rations have been pretty good since coming off the front. It's surely nice to be getting hot meals again for a change. One gets awfully tired of cold rations – no doubt lots of the men will acquire stomach trouble in years to come. I've always had a pretty strong stomach so I don't think it will bother me very much.

    Very soon now I may be seeing you. I have hopes of it anyway. I sincerely believe I've seen my last combat. Maybe by the time the lilacs bloom again I'll be home.

Love,
Orlie

Dear Folks, Love Orlie

▼

Somewhere in Italy

March 2, 1944

Dear Folks,

Sorry I haven't written oftener these past few days but I've been pretty busy. I've a lot of work getting my company reorganized for combat again. I'm getting replacements now so they keep me pretty busy. Then too I had to testify at a general court martial today. One of my men was charged with desertion and I had to testify against him. They were asking for the maximum penalty and I guess you know what that is. I don't know yet what he got. I really couldn't blame the poor devil very much – Cassino was a blazing hell. His nerves were pretty badly shot. I'm a little shaky myself yet. I narrowly missed death dozens of times myself. It will take a long time to erase that battle from my mind. We killed plenty of Germans though so maybe our extremely heavy casualties are justified. If they would have bombed the Abbey sooner more men would be alive today. I was in favor of bombing it if it would save just one American life – to hell with the Germans – the only way I like them is the way they look dead – black and stiff.

It's been raining here for the past week – never really seems to stop. Surely glad we're off the front. The British boys are in Cassino now. The British boys we meet down here are a bunch of good "Joe's" – much better than those we met in England and Ireland. They're darned good soldiers – lots of "guts" and stubborn as hell.

The furniture Bernice sent you should look nice

after some paint. I've been away so long it's hard for me to remember lots of things. One of the things I remember awfully well is the comical expression little Jeep gets on his face when he's a little peeved. He could never take the place of old Pal but he comes pretty close. Guess I loved Pal so much because he sort of grew up with me. It still brings a lump to my throat when I think of the good times we had together. Guess war still hasn't made me too bitter – I still look forward to hunting and fishing trips with Jeep, working with flowers, my old pipes, a home of my own and my first boy.

I'm getting quite a good lot of mail these days. Seems like I get at least one letter every day. I've several other letters to write tonight but thought I'd write to you first because I may get tired and I wanted to be sure and get a letter to you tonight. I've got to write to John Curries' folks and his brother. He was the fellow who got killed in Africa.

Timmins is here in my tent tonight. He's about the only old man I have left. I had some of the others reclassified because they were mentally and physically unfit for more combat duty. Most of them were battle neurosis cases. Mild shell shock in other words. Poor devils, I feel sorry for them – but they may be better off than I am.

Well, folks, guess I'll close for this time. I'll write again soon. Write when you can.

Love,
Orlie

Dear Folks, Love Orlie

▼

Somewhere in Italy

March 7, 1944

Dear Folks,

Just a few lines to let you know I'm okay and thinking of you. Your mail has been coming through pretty good lately. In fact, I've been getting letters from lots of people. I've had letters from you, Jo Popenhagen, Junior Reynolds and several others. Keeps me pretty busy trying to answer all of them.

The weather here has been rather changeable. One moment the sun is shining and then it starts to rain. Typical spring weather I should say. It's glorious when the sun shines and not too bad when it rains. A few little flowers similar to our butter cups are springing up.

I'm still in a rest area. It surely seems nice to be able to lay down and know you're not going to be shelled out of your bed before morning. Then, too, you don't have to lie in a fox hole that's half full of water. It's awfully nice to be able to get a bath and clean, fresh clothes.

I've been seeing some pretty good stage shows and movies since I got here. Of course, we have an open air theater but we enjoy them very much nevertheless. I always was pretty much of a movie fiend. That's one big thing La-Vonne and I have in common. She very rarely misses any of the good shows.

By the way, you asked about Dick Emery. I have him reported as missing in action. I think he was probably wounded and then captured. As I look back over the situation and think of the terrain I don't see how he could have been captured without being wounded. We made a daylight attack over wide open ground. We ran into heavy machine gun and mortar fire – there was very heavy casualties and I think Dick must have been one of them. The Germans beat off our attack and probably picked up most of our wounded that night. I'm positive he wasn't killed because we drove them from their positions later and I personally looked at all our dead and Dick wasn't among them. Of course, some of the bodies were pretty badly mutilated but I think I could have identified almost any part of him.

    Well, folks, guess I'd better close for this time. Keep up the good work – the writing I mean. I'll write again soon.

Love, Orlie

Dear Folks, Love Orlie

> March 10, 1944 – The Regiment moved to San Giorgio, near Benevento, where replacements were received and a period of intensive training resulted.

―――――――――▼―――――――――

March 12, 1944

Dear Folks,

Received three letters from you today and one from Bob. Of course you know he's at the Beachhead. He talked like things were okay though. I believe the pressure is off up there now and the Yanks will make progress. All of your letters were postmarked late in February.

I knew about Homer before you told me but I just wasn't saying anything. I thought it best to let the war department take care of that. He was killed in the battle for Cassino. Tell his folks that I'm awfully sorry and wish there was some way I could help. You can also tell his folks he was one of the finest soldiers I know. His combat record was extremely high – had several Germans to his credit. After a guy kills the first one the rest come easy. We talked about that the last time we were together. Homer made the supreme sacrifice – that's all anyone can ask. He did what all of us are ready to do – laid down his life for his country and those he loved. No matter what the people thought of Dill and him he rates tops with me – in my mind he's just another infantry boy who lost his life.

We of the infantry stick awfully close together – after all's said and done it's the old infantry who decides every battle through mud, rain, blood, tears and guts. There will never be another soldier who compares to the tried and true dough foot.

We have made another move. We are now about 100 miles back of the front. We're back here for replacements and training. We lost about 7,705 casualties at Cassino. I still have Olson, Timmins, Gardner and Foster of the original 123 men. So you can see what my outfit is like and beside that I've probably had and used 300 replacements. I had 9 fellows hurt and two killed by one shell at Cassino. Seven of the 9 wounded will be cripples.

The weather here now is pretty nice. It's much greener here than it was further north. The farmers are sowing grain and everything looks fairly prosperous. Well, folks, guess I'll close for this time. Write often.

Love, Orlie

> March 16, 1944 – The 2nd Bn., which had been on guard duty at AFHQ in North Africa, rejoined the Regiment. The 100th Bn. was relieved of assignment to the 133rd Infantry but remained attached up to 31 March.

Dear Folks, Love Orlie

▼

Somewhere in Italy

March 21, 1944

Dear Folks,

Just a few lines to let you know I'm okay and thinking of you. Sorry I haven't been writing oftener but I know you understand. I've been awfully busy these past two weeks getting my outfit ready for the next combat phase. We're doing combat training now as we always do in our rest periods. Battalion defense problems, night assaults, counter-attack tactics, and all types of tactics, both defensive and offensive.

Censorship regulations have relaxed enough according to a late memorandum I just received that we can now describe some of our experiences. I'll try to go over some of the things that have happened here in Italy. I've been in about 15 engagements – 6 major and 9 minor. Of the lot Cassino was undoubtedly the worst I've ever seen. When we landed we walked nearly 70 miles before we contacted the enemy and even then it was only small clashes. Our first big operation was the crossing of the Volturno River. "Jerry" had every type of fire known to modern warfare ranged in to the extent that he could place immediate fire on any sector to their front. We crossed in spite of this fire and drove "Jerry" from his positions.

The next major battle was the battle on the "pool table". We like to call it the pool table because the terrain was absolutely flat. We were attacking two battalions in depth. Our mission was to attack swiftly and viciously through the leading battalion as soon as it was pinned down. When this happened it was foggy and extremely bad for a night attack. The Germans infiltrated through our lines and generally caused trouble. At the same time enemy tanks attacked in force. In the end we again gave Jerry the wrong end of the stick and killed lots of them. When the fog lifted we ferreted out the machine gun nests and snipers and finished them off in a very permanent fashion. This was one of the times when American envelopment tactics and German infiltration tactics caused plenty of trouble to both units.

The next big offensive engagement was when we crossed the Volturno for the third and last time. We had little difficulty in crossing the river but before we gained our objective we ran into intense German fire of all types. My company commander was killed in the ensuing action and so were many others of my outfit. This was the battle where my helmet saved my life. If it hadn't have been for my helmet a piece of fragment would have entered my head just behind my left ear. We obtained our objective, however, in spite of "Jerry's" numerous counter attacks.

Then came Cassino! A blazing hell is the most fitting description. There were dozens of times when I wondered if I'd ever see Shellsburg again. In those times, it's funny how a person's mind wanders. I remembered so many of my boyhood days. Fishing trips with Pal, my first girl, swimming and, most of all, George Thompson and I playing war. Guess Dad never enjoyed our war games – the garden was usually left in a miserable state.

Well, folks, I'll close for this time. Give my regards to everyone.

Love, Orlie

Dear Folks, Love Orlie

▼

Somewhere in Italy

April 19, 1944

Dear Folks,

Just a few lines to pass some good news on to you – I'm on my way home! I have been selected for rotation and maybe I'll be home before this letter – at least shortly after. So get the fried chicken, potato salad and etc. ready. I had hoped to be home by Mother's Day but I rather doubt if I will make it.

Don't write anymore letters because I'm not with my old outfit now. In fact, I haven't been with them for nearly a month.

I'm going to try to arrange for LaVonne to stay with us during my furlough -- perhaps I'll even marry her while I'm home. Of course, when we see each other again we may decide it's no go. In that case, I'll just have to spend my time locating another one.

Well, folks, guess I'll have to close for this time. This will be the last letter before I get home. I'll wire you when I get to the States. Tell everyone hello and that I'll be seeing them soon.

Love, Orlie

Orlie Meskimen

▼

Somewhere in Italy

April 29, 1944

Dear Folks,

It seems I may not be home as soon as I expected. Naturally I can't tell you the reason why. I'm safe though and will not see combat again before I see you and that's one consolation.

I'm sure I will see you sometime within the next month or so. Very probably it will be June. Look around and see if I have any fishing tackle around.

I just came back from a movie. I see a movie or stage show every night at the Red Cross camp theater. Everything is fine with me. I don't do a thing but play baseball, eat, sleep and see shows. I'll have to crack down again when I'm assigned to a new outfit in the States!

Love, Orlie

Orlie is listed as participating in the following engagements in Italy:
- Montemiletto, September 30, 1943
- Benevento, October 2-3, 1943
- 2nd crossing of Volturno River, October 19, 1943
- Alife, October 20, 1943
- St. Angelo d'Alife, October 20-23, 1943
- Ciaralno, October 31 – November 3, 1943
- St. Maria Aliveto, November 3-11, 1943
- Mt. Marrone, November 25 – December 10, 1943
- Engagement of Monte Cassino, January 1 – February 21, 1944

JUNE 1944
RETURN TO THE STATES

Following the horrible battle at Monte Cassino, and with his mental and physical health compromised, Orlie was selected for rotation and shipped back to the states in May/June 1944. His military records state that he was considered unfit for continued overseas assignment due to combat reaction being moderately severe. It is noted that he was treated twice for malaria while serving in Africa, first in September and again in November of 1943.

―――――― ▼ ――――――

Camp Butler, North Carolina

June 15, 1944

Dear Folks,

    Arrived here okay and on time. I didn't leave Cedar Rapids until 0400 o'clock because my train was late but I still made good connections and got here in plenty of time.

    The weather here is awfully hot but at the present time

it's raining so of course it's cool now. I'm glad I don't stay at this camp because I know I wouldn't like it. I will be here about a week or a little more probably. You can use this address until I give you another.

Did you make it home okay with the car? Here are some of the things I want done to it: 2 new tires, grease job, upholstery cleaned and see if you can find a bumper jack.

I may be getting a furlough sooner than I thought. Don't plan on anything before fall but it's possible that I may be home this summer yet.

I met Fred Oyler and Armstrong in Cedar Rapids so the three of us made the trip down here together. Since I've been here about all I've done is write letters. Of course, I haven't even had much time for that. I've written to LaVonne, Diane, and you folks.

They are surely treating us good here. We have about 3 days processing and from there on we only have to report back each day at 0500 o'clock. The rest of the time we can spend in town. We will take mental and physical tests. I'm going to try to be assigned to a northern camp. Don't know just how much good I will be able to do but it's worth a try.

Well, folks, guess I'll have to close for this time. Write when you can and I'll write as often as possible.

Love,
Orlie

Dear Folks, Love Orlie

▼

Camp Butler, North Carolina

July, 1944

1st page of letter is missing ...

... the old way and I know from combat experience that much of the old way is no good. We've had several pretty hot arguments already.

I was awfully sorry to hear about Louie Popenhagen. Those things happen in war though and they must be expected. Extend my sincerest sympathy to the Popenhagens.

The 4th was a day of duty for me but I'm used to not celebrating holidays so it didn't make much difference. I have one afternoon a week off and of course Sunday's.

Well, folks, I'll have to close for this time. Write when you can. If you ever get a chance try and have those fenders straightened and repainted. I won't be home this fall so have prestone put in and the heater checked.

Love,
Orlie

July 1944 – Camp Blanding, Florida

July 22, 1944

Dear Folks,

Just a few lines to let you know I'm okay and thinking of you. I've been out on bivouac (maneuvers) this past week and will be all next week. That's the reason I haven't been writing. I've been pretty busy so haven't had much time to write. I only have two more weeks in this cycle and then I will be getting 200 more new men fresh from the farms and factories. I'll be glad to get rid of these fellows and get a new bunch that I can start training right from the start. I may be transferred to another company in the battalion in the next two or three weeks. I surely hope so because I can't get along with the company commander I have in this company.

I have been getting quite a lot of mail since I came to this camp. I think my mail is pretty well caught up now. I get quite a lot of mail from LaVonne and Diane now – guess they're a little afraid one of them will get ahead of the other. Reynolds writes to me sometimes about twice a day. I'm not going to let either one of them get any ideas about me. Reynolds wants to visit me down here but there's no place she could stay. So many of the Army men have their wives down here that all available facilities are in use. I don't think I want either one of them down here anyway because I'm so busy.

The news surely sounds good, doesn't it? I don't think old Hitler has very long to last. I think the war with Germany will be over by the first of the year. Revolutions are starting in Germany and they are very definitely against the Hitler gang. He's purged some of his best generals in the past few days and that proves that things could be better in the German Army. According to reports from neutral countries the German people are starting to revolt too. The end is definitely in sight for Hitler and all that he stands for.

It's rained here everyday for the past week or so. They can talk all they want to about sunny Florida but I've yet to see very much sun. The natives say this weather is very unusual for this time of year. Usually it doesn't rain very much except during the winter months. I'll surely be glad to get out of the south when this war is over. I'm going to try to come home on furlough around Christmas time but don't know just yet how I will come out. It's going to be pretty difficult to get a furlough from here. They are so busy down here training new men that they can't spare a man. Incidentally, you asked me what "Cadre" meant – it's a group of experienced men who are used to train other men who have not had that experience. Most of them are overseas returnee's.

Well, folks, guess I'll have to close for this time. I've got to take a group of men out on a combat machine gun range and teach them the fundamentals of overhead fire. It's pretty dangerous for these new men – some of them get a little excited when the bullets start to fly over

Orlie Meskimen

their heads and as a consequence they get hurt. I'll write again as soon as I have time. At times I'll be so busy or so tired that I won't be able to write but I'll be thinking of you. Tell everyone hello for me.

Love,

Orlie

Dear Folks, Love Orlie

▼

Camp Blanding, Florida

July 26, 1944

Dear Folks,

Received two letters from you a few days ago and was so glad to hear from you. I'm sorry I haven't been writing oftener but I've been so awfully busy I just can't seem to find time to write. As soon as this bivouac is over I'll be able to write more often.

By the way, I want you to send me the following addresses – Tom Fish, Earl, Don and Bunky. I've lost all of them. I'll be glad to write to all of them because I know how important mail is to the fellows overseas.

We had a little rain today but I think the rainy spell is nearly over. I'm beginning to like my work better too so guess I really haven't got such a bad deal here at all. I have my own office with just two desks – one for me and one for my clerk. My sleeping quarters are excellent and the food couldn't be better. I should put on some weight down here after the weather cools off a little bit. The camp itself has very good recreational facilities – nice canteens, good theaters, guest houses, bowling alleys, service clubs and good transportation to the nearby large towns (Jacksonville and St. Augustine).

I got a nice letter from Mrs. Emery. I wrote to her about Dick. She said John made the landing on France "D" day. Bet John is a good combat soldier.

Well, folks, guess this is all for this time. Write again soon. I'd like to have some pictures of the car.

Love, Orlie

Orlie Meskimen

▼

Camp Blanding, Florida

August 1, 1944

Dear Folks,

    I'm awfully sorry I haven't written oftener but I'm so busy. When I finally get my work done I'm so tired I'm ready for bed. I'll try to do better in the future though.

    I had a nice letter from Bob Bergen a few days ago. He gave me a little hell for going with Diane again but said he guessed I was old enough to know what I was doing. Everyone seems to jump to a lot of conclusions about me when in reality they don't really know what the score is. I sometimes wonder if I know myself.

    It's raining as usual here tonight. It rains sometime every day. The rainy season should soon be over with though. The days are getting cooler now and the nights are perfect for sleeping.

    I'm back in camp again after the bivouac I wrote about in my last letter. Seems good to be back here again. I've done too much camping out in the past two years to enjoy it anymore.

    I'd like to have some pictures of my car if you can ever get any film. Guess the one of me standing beside it didn't turn out, did it? I'd surely like to have it down here with me but guess there's no way to get it here.

    I'm well acquainted now and have made some very good friends. There's one overseas returnee in my company

Dear Folks, Love Orlie

who came home from Italy – he was in Bob's division – the 45th. There are quite a number of 34th boys here too. I'm getting along much better with my company commander now. In fact, we're pretty thick.

I've had a few dates since I've been here – met two really nice girls. I don't get out more than once a week, so naturally don't have much of an opportunity to get around. I get a kick out of these southern gals. Reynolds had me "snowed" for awhile but now Butler is in the driver's seat.

Well, folks, guess I'll have to close for this time. Write often.

Love,
Orlie
P.S. I'm enclosing some negatives I found. Have them printed and send me the one where I'm sitting with a sailor.

Orlie Meskimen

▼

Camp Blanding, Florida

August 8, 1944

Dear Folks,

Well, tonight is a cool, pleasant night. Thought I'd drop you a few lines to let you know I'm okay and thinking of you. I haven't heard from you for several days but I guess you're busy just as me.

It rained early in the evening and now it's awfully cool and nice. Should be a very good night for sleeping. I've got to write two more letters tonight so I guess I'll be ready for bed by the time I get finished. I've got to write to LaVonne B. and Bob Bergen.

I just came back from a movie a little while ago. I have a camp theater within 2 blocks of my barracks so I have my entertainment handy. They have a different movie every night and a matinee on Sunday. I don't get to go every night but I go every time I'm not busy. It's relaxing and then too, I enjoy movies.

I got your letter with Don's and Earl's addresses and I'll write to them as soon as I have time. I think an awful lot of all of Oscar's kids. Louise and Elmer tried awfully hard to help me have a good time. I'm afraid I wasn't very good company for anyone. I was so restless and nervous. I certainly like Elmer though – he's a swell guy.

Well, folks, guess this will have to be all for this time. Write to me when you can. Tell everyone hello for me.

Love, Orlie

Dear Folks, Love Orlie

▼

Camp Blanding, Florida

August 14, 1944

Dear Folks,

Just a few lines to let you know I'm okay and thinking of you. I got two letters from you over the weekend. Also one from LaVonne B. She wants to meet me in Iowa at Christmas time and get married – I might take her up on it. She's bound and determined that I become a Catholic though and that's the only drawback. Wants me to promise that I'd let our children be Catholics at any rate. It's not that I have anything against them, it's just the idea that I'd have to turn Catholic in order to marry a girl. I'm giving it serious thought though and may decide to send her a ring soon.

Seeing Diane again was really good for me. It settled a lot of things between her and I that no one else knew anything about. She's really a good kid and I'll always think an awful lot of her. Nobody ever understood us and as a result both of us were misjudged and wrongfully talked about. It took a lot of courage for her to do what she did. Maybe if people had let us alone and tried to understand us things would have been different now. She's a grand little person and I'll always have the highest regard and respect for her.

I feel awfully bad about Jack Peterman. These things must be expected in war though. There will be more from Shellsburg. Jack had a pretty miserable sort of life. Seems like someone else whose life had been fuller would have been selected. War knows no accidents though and neither does God.

Well, folks, guess I'll have to close for this time. Write when you can. Tell everyone hello for me. I'll write a letter to Peterman's.

Love,
Orlie

Dear Folks, Love Orlie

▼

Camp Blanding, Florida

August 22, 1944

Dear Folks,

Just a few lines to let you know I'm okay and thinking of you. I'm sorry I haven't been writing oftener but I've been pretty busy and just haven't had time. I'm getting caught up on a little of my work now so maybe I'll be able to write more often in the future. I've been getting lots of mail so I'm pretty much behind in my letter writing too. I owe about 10 letters now.

I want you to send me $100 by return mail. You can get a money order for it. Five of us are going to buy us a car down here so we can do a little running around on weekends. We can't lose anything on it and it's practically impossible to get around otherwise. I've started to pal around with four of my Sergeants. They're darned nice fellows – three of them are overseas returnee's. Send me the money by return mail so we can have the car this weekend. I plan to take a little trip to Pensacola to visit Roger one of these days.

I haven't written to Peterman's yet but will as soon as I can find time. They have surely had a lot of trouble. Jack must have turned out to be a pretty good soldier. It isn't easy to get promoted to a Sergeant. I always thought a lot of Jack even if he was a little crazy at times. Jack was a good kid at heart and was pretty well liked around Shellsburg. He and Louis Popenhagen used to run around quite a lot together. Seems odd that both of them had to get it.

The weather here the past week has been much better. It's cooled off considerably and there is a nice breeze. I've been doing a little swimming and would like to find time to do more. There are some awfully nice places to swim down here. There is one lake right here in camp that covers about 40 acres so you can see that it's pretty good sized. I'm making so many mistakes that you probably won't be able to read this. It's been so long since I did much typing that I'm a little rusty at it.

I suppose the canning factory is in full swing just now. Did they have much corn out this year? I used to have a lot of fun working up there. Old Dutch Gillis was usually drunk so there was always some excitement around. I always kind of liked Dutch in spite of all of his bad points.

Well, I guess I'd better close for this time. I'll try to write again soon. I haven't been doing much getting around down here. I've taken about 8 or 10 different women out since I've been here but haven't found any I'm particularly interested in as yet. I've never liked southern girls especially well. But it gives a guy something to do. Write when you can. Tell everyone hello for me.

Love,
Orlie

Dear Folks, Love Orlie

▼

Camp Blanding, Florida

August 29, 1944

Dear Folks,

Just a few lines to let you know I'm okay and thinking of you. I got a letter from you yesterday. I also got the money order in plenty of time so we were able to have the car over the weekend. We bought a 1937 Plymouth. It's in excellent shape but isn't a very good looking car. It runs darned good so I guess we shouldn't complain. We went down to Coral Gables and also Silver Springs. There are springs there 60 feet long. They have lots of alligators down there too. It's much nicer country down there than it is here around Camp Blanding. It's about 150 miles down south of here. We plan to go to Miami sometime if we can get a three day pass.

LaVonne Butler and I plan to be married around Christmas time if I can manage to get a furlough at that time. She will come to Cedar Rapids and we will be married there. I've made up my mind beyond even the slightest doubt. I really don't mind the Catholic end of things. I've always been pretty broad minded about such things. I'm not going to turn Catholic but I've agreed to let any children we might have be Catholics. Diane and I don't even write to each other anymore. We're not mad at each other we just decided that it wasn't any use. I don't mind if you tell people about LaVonne Butler and I. We've definitely decided that we're going to be married.

Orlie Meskimen

The weather down here is a little better now. It isn't quite as hot as it was. The nights are getting better for sleeping now too. For about two weeks it was so hot I could hardly sleep. I've got a beautiful tan. From my waist up and also my legs. We've started a new cycle so I have lots of time now. I do a lot of swimming. I go nearly every evening. I've gained nearly ten pounds since I've been here and my nerves have quieted down considerably.

The news surely sounds good, doesn't it? I believe the krauts will be finished sometime in October if not before. They are going to discharge between one and two million men when Germany falls. Men with long periods of service and the most combat duty will be given priority. I might stand a pretty good chance. I'm sure as hell going to try to get out. I'm awfully fed up with the way they run the Army here in the States. Guess I'll have to close for this time.

Love,
Orlie

Dear Folks, Love Orlie

▼

Camp Blanding, Florida
September 2, 1944
Dear Folks,

Sorry I haven't been writing oftener but it seems I'm always busy and then too, I'm pretty tired when night comes. I'll try to write often enough that you will know I'm okay. Your mail has been coming through in good shape. I'm getting so many letters that it's hard for me to keep up my correspondence.

This month makes me wish I was home. I'd like to get in on a little of the squirrel hunting. But I'll be home sometime this fall and can take Jeep out then. All furloughs are frozen now and I surely hope they lift that restriction before Christmas time. If it should happen that I can't get a furlough LaVonne is coming down here.

I want you to send me all the money I have over $1,000 there at home. I want to put it in soldier's savings. They pay 4% straight interest and the money isn't earning anything for me there at home. Then you can send me the allotment money each month as you get it. If I keep $1,000 there all the time it will act as sort of an emergency fund. You can send it in money orders. I'd like to have it as soon as possible so I can get the interest going. Another good point about this soldier's savings is that you can't get the money until you are discharged.

The weather is beginning to cool off a little down here now. By the end of this month it should be fairly decent. The heat doesn't bother me very much anymore except that I get heat rash but most of the fellows do. It hasn't been raining so much lately as it did for awhile.

LaVonne is bound and determined that she will come down here after we've married. I agree with her. There's no use of us getting married if we can't be with each other. I can find a nice apartment for her. She wants to work and that's alright too. It will give her something to do during the day. There is plenty of work for soldier's wives right here in camp. It would also help with the financial end. I don't like to go into my savings anymore than I absolutely have to. Another thing – she wants an addition just as soon as possible. Guess I'll see what I can do about it.

I got a very nice letter from Mrs. Reynolds several days ago. I like her but I'm not overly crazy about Mark. I think she was trying to pump me about Diane and I. We haven't written to each other for over a month now.

Well, folks, I guess I'll have to close for this time. Write when you can and I'll do the same. Tell everyone hello for me.

Love,
Orlie

Dear Folks, Love Orlie

▼

Camp Blanding, Florida

September 25, 1944

Dear Folks,

This will be just a few lines to let you know I'm okay and thinking of you. I got the money order okay and plan to go in for the ring tomorrow or the next day. LaVonne says she would rather wait until we're together so we can pick one out together. Maybe she is right. I'm going to wait a few more days and see what she says in her next letter.

The weather here today is surely nice. Feels almost like fall weather in Iowa. It's cloudy and there's a swell cool breeze blowing. Seems like I'd ought to be going squirrel hunting. There are lots of squirrels down here but they don't have an open season on them. I plan to do a little duck hunting later on.

I didn't go anywhere over the weekend. I was pretty tired so I spent the weekend here in camp. Slept nearly all day Sunday. The days are getting cool enough now that a person can sleep in the afternoons. We're getting up at 4 o'clock now so I really get sleepy before the day is over. I usually manage to get a couple of hours sleep sometime during the day. The company goes to the field at 6 o'clock in the morning each day so there are only about a dozen of us in the company area during the days.

I have written to Earl Mason. I wrote about two weeks ago. He should be getting the letter before so very much longer. I'll write to Don as soon as I have time. I'm so darned busy all the time that it's hard for me to find time to write to anyone.

I've been getting lots of mail the past two or three weeks. I'm so far behind in my letter writing that I don't think I'll ever get caught up again. I'm going to try and write some letters tonight if I possibly can.

I don't know just when I'll be able to get a furlough. I may have to take one before the holidays. If I do I plan to take it in November.

Well, folks, guess I'll have to close for this time. I'll write more later. Write when you can.

Love,
Orlie

Dear Folks, Love Orlie

▼

Camp Blanding, Florida

October 6, 1944

Dear Folks,

This will be just a few short lines to let you know I'm okay and thinking of you. I'm sorry I haven't been writing oftener but I've been so busy that I just haven't had time. I haven't been feeling any good either. I'm having some trouble with my throat too. The doctors say it's acute laryngitis. It will soon clear up now, though it isn't nearly as sore as it was several days ago.

We're having a company party here tonight. We're having a chicken supper with beer afterwards. It should be fun if I felt a little better.

Since I've been down here I've been awarded the combat infantry badge for exceptional combat ability. It pays me $10 more a month so I'm not at all mad about the whole deal. It also gives me a rather nice feeling. The badge is a blue bar with a rifle in the center and a wreath around the whole thing.

I'd like to have you send me another $50 because I'm out of money. The finance section screwed me up this time and I only drew $7. I put the last hundred you sent me in soldier's savings because LaVonne and I decided that we wouldn't have an engagement ring. She wants just a nice wedding ring. She also wants it to be a double ring ceremony. She says she wants me to wear a gold band so other women will understand that I'm already taken. If it happens that I can't get home before Christmas or at Christmas time she's going to come down here and we'll be married here in Florida. She says that if I go back to school we won't be able to start a family right away. I guess she's right at that.

You will have to excuse my stationary. It's all I have at the moment. I notice that this sheet has been mimeographed on the back but it didn't come out very good.

The weather here now is much better. It's still pretty hot during the days but it gets nice and cool at night. We won't go into wools until about the end of next month so you can see that fall comes pretty late down here. The trees keep their leaves all winter too. There aren't very many palm trees around here but about fifty miles south of here it's almost like the tropics. We went down to Miami over the weekend and had a very good time. The car we have runs very good. We haven't had a bit of trouble with it yet.

I've written to Earl and I'll write to Don just as soon as I have time. It's a funny thing that Don should be so anxious to hear from me. He sure as hell never wrote very much to me when I was overseas and he was here in the States but I'll write anyway.

Well, folks, guess I'll have to close for this time. Write when you can and I'll do the same. Tell everyone hello for me. I've got to write a letter to LaVonne as soon as I finish this. I haven't written to her for over a week.

Love,
Orlie

Dear Folks, Love Orlie

▼

Camp Blanding, Florida

October 16, 1944

Dear Folks,

This will be just a few short lines to tell you my furlough was cancelled so I won't be home when I thought I would. Moreover I don't think I will be able to get one until well after the first of the year. All overseas returnee's must be in this camp over six months before they are eligible for furloughs. I guess LaVonne will just have to come down here later on. I don't know what to do about my car. I'll need it when LaVonne gets here. I guess I'll have to have you ship it down. I think it will cost about $150 but it can't be helped. I wish you would check on the details and let me know as soon as possible. I think she will be able to come about the end of this month or the first of next. If I had more money I'd buy one down here but I think it will be cheaper to have the Mercury shipped down. I think Sam Whorley can give you all the details on it. You would have to be sure that all the papers are in the glove compartment. All the tires could be put in the trunk. I hate to take it away from you folks but there just doesn't seem to be any other way. About the nearest town that I'll be able to put LaVonne in is about 30 miles away. I'll be able to get gas enough to drive back and forth every night.

The weather here is very chilly and miserable. It's been that way all weekend. It's typical fall weather. Rain's nearly all the time. I have a pretty nasty cold but it's beginning to clear up a little bit now.

    I haven't heard from you for about four or five days now but will probably get a letter today. I owe so many letters that it's doubtful if I'll ever get caught up again. I'm going to try to write a few letters this evening but I know I'll never get all of them written that I should.

    I didn't do anything over the weekend because it was so cold and miserable. Most of the places down here don't have any heat whatsoever so there isn't much fun in going anywhere when it's so cold.

    Well, folks, I guess I'll have to close for this time. I've got some paper work that I have to get out right away. I'll try to write again soon. I'll be waiting for the details on sending the car down. I'll have a lot of running around to do before LaVonne gets down here. Hope I have good luck finding an apartment. If we can get two rooms I think that will be enough. Write when you can.

Love, Orlie

Dear Folks, Love Orlie

▼

Camp Blanding, Florida

October 23, 1944

Dear Folks,

This will be just a few short lines to let you know I'm okay and thinking of you. I got a letter from you yesterday and also one from LaVonne. Bernard (LaVonne's brother) is home from overseas so we may put off our marriage until after the first of the year. He is in the hospital out where LaVonne is. He has a rather severe case of malaria and will probably be in the hospital for about thirty days. It will make it better for me all around. I'd rather come home to marry her and I won't be able to get a furlough until after the first of the year. There is some talk around here that all overseas returnees are going to get Christmas furloughs. As far as I know though it's still just a rumor. Most of the fellows here in this camp from overseas haven't been home for Christmas for about three years. This will be my fourth year if I don't make it. Don't plan on anything though because it's just a rumor as far as I'm concerned. Personally I don't see how they can spare all of us at that time. About seventy percent of all the cadre are overseas returnees right now.

The weather here has got very cold again. I have the top to my woolen underwear on this morning. They haven't given us authorization to start fires in the stoves in our huts yet either so it's pretty chilly at night. We go into wool uniforms the thirty first of this month and it won't be a darned bit too soon. I don't have an overcoat yet but I'll surely have to have one. As soon as we go into wools I'm going to have some pictures made in town.

About the car. I'm going to let it go for the present and see how things work out. I may just wait and drive it down. As far as buying a car down here goes you can't buy one of any sort for less than $500. You would be able to buy one considerably cheaper up there. When I come home on furlough I'll go to Cedar Rapids with Dad and help him buy one.

I got a nice letter a couple of days ago from one of the fellows in the old 133rd. A lot more of the fellows I knew have been killed or wounded. The fellow sitting at the table with Dick Emery and me has been killed. His name was McDougle. I think you have the picture there. We were all smoking cigars and drinking beer. He was an awfully nice guy and a very good friend of mine. We were known as the Three Musketeers. The three of us used to run around together all the time.

Well it looks like I'll have to close for this time because I'm about out of paper. I'm typing nearly all my letters now because it's so much faster. I make a lot of mistakes but I guess you are able to make them out. By the way, did you ever take any pictures of the car? I'm very anxious to have some pictures of it so try and send me some. One of the fellows in the company has one just like it except that it's maroon color. It isn't in nearly as good a shape as mine though. Tell everyone hello for me.

Love, Orlie

Dear Folks, Love Orlie

▼

Camp Blanding, Florida
October 26, 1944
Dear Folks,

This will be just a few lines to let you know I'm okay and thinking of you. I haven't heard from you for several days but will probably get a letter today. I'm about caught up on my letter writing now. I thought I'd never get all the letters written that I should. I still owe the Popenhagen's a letter. Guess I'll write it as soon as I finish this one. I have a few idle moments now so guess I'd better get it done while I have a chance.

It's a beautiful day here today. The sun is out for the first time in several days and it's surely a welcome relief after all the gray weather we've been having. The hurricane missed us by a few miles. We were all prepared for it anyway. We rolled full field packs and were all set to take off for the wide open spaces if it had come this way. We got some strong wind out of the deal but nothing really serious. It blew down some small buildings but nothing that really amounted to very much. I guess it caused considerable damage in some parts of the state though.

There's a very good rumor spreading around here now. I don't know just how much basis there is but it at least sounds good. They say that they are soon going to start examining overseas returnees for discharge and those who are in the best physical condition will be released. They will not be subject to draft but the Army can recall them at anytime if an emergency exists. I'm awfully anxious to get out because I'm pretty well fed up with the way they run things around here. There seems to be no system whatsoever in any of the procedures in this camp.

I got a nice letter from one of the fellows in the old outfit yesterday. They're still plugging away at the Krauts. Guess they will never let the old 34th rest. I'm certainly proud that I was in that outfit. I was reading in the Infantry Journal that it is classed as the best infantry division in the American Army. That's saying quite a lot. Several of the old gang have been wounded or killed since the last letter I got from them. This is the second letter I've gotten from them this week.

I got another letter from Mrs. Reynolds yesterday too. She just wanted to wish me luck and said that all of them were holding their breaths hoping that Diane and I would get back together again. I don't think I'll answer it at all. Mrs. Reynolds is a nice person and has always been good to me. They found out somehow that LaVonne and I were going to get married and she wanted to wish me luck.

Well, folks, I guess I'd better close for this time. I'll try to write more in the next few days. It seems I never get caught up enough in my work to write very many letters. I'm not as busy now as I was several weeks ago but I still have enough to do.

Love,
Orlie

Dear Folks, Love Orlie

▼

Camp Blanding, Florida
November, 1944
Dear Folks,

    I got your latest letter along with the pictures of the car. They are all good. I'm glad you stood close to the car because it makes a better picture that way. It surely shines with the sun on it. Looks pretty sharp.

    I hate to ask you to send me more money but I need a hundred dollars just as soon as you can send it to me. One of the fellows I bought this car with is being sent overseas and one of us will have to buy his share. I'm the only one who has any money at all so I guess I'm it. I may buy the whole thing sooner or later. It would make a nice car for you folks. I should be able to get it for about $350 or somewhere around that. Send me the money by return mail. I'll need it by Friday or Saturday. I think this fellow is leaving about Saturday.

    I didn't do much this weekend. Went to a football game Saturday afternoon. It wasn't much of a game but something to pass the time. It was a game between two of the local high schools. It's getting cool enough now that there isn't much doing at the beaches. I used to go there every weekend but nobody goes now so there isn't much to do.

    I haven't heard from LaVonne for more than a week but I guess she's pretty busy and excited now that her brother is home. She surely thinks a lot of him. She seems to worry a lot about him when she knows he's in a combat zone.

Well, folks, I guess I'll have to close for this time. Send me the money by return mail. Tell everyone hello for me.

Love,

Orlie

Dear Folks, Love Orlie

▼

Camp Blanding, Florida

November 16, 1944

Dear Folks,

Just a few lines to let you know I'm okay and thinking of you. I got the money and it got here just in time. It came in the mail Saturday afternoon and the fellow was leaving that evening. I now own one half of the car and the fellows will be shipping soon so perhaps I'll own all of it before very long. It's in excellent running condition and could be made into a pretty nice looking car. About all it needs is a paint job. It's nice and clean inside too.

I've had a pretty nasty cold the past few days but it's much better now. I had to take a physical yesterday and they dropped me down lower one grade than I was. They classified me "Combat reaction, moderately severe" – I guess they mean I'm still having a nervous reaction. I have a little trouble with my nerves but as far as I'm concerned it doesn't bother.

The weather here now is very nice. It's just cool enough to be really nice. Wool clothes are just right for the time being. The weather is so darned changeable that you never know just what to put on in the morning. They have a few grouse down here and I'm going hunting for them this weekend.

I haven't heard from LaVonne for nearly two weeks but I guess she is pretty excited about Bernard being home so I'm not going to say anything to her about it. I haven't written to her for nearly that long either. She owes me a letter so I'm going to wait until she writes to me before I write to her.

Things look very good in Europe now, don't they? I believe that if they put enough pressure on the Germans they can whip them by sometime next summer. People are much too optimistic about the war with Germany. She is still a very strong nation. I know the Jerry's – they will fight until the last German is either wounded or killed. They can talk all they want about the Japs but they will never hold a candle to the Germans when it comes to war. With the Germans it's a business and one that they have been schooled in to the highest degree. With the Japs it's fanatical but they're not clever like the Germans nor do they have the weapons the Germans have.

Well, folks, I guess I'd better close for this time. I've got some paper work that I've got to have in in about two hours and it will keep both myself and my clerk pretty busy to get it ready. He's working at it now but it will take both of us to get it ready. Write when you can. Tell everyone hello for me.

Love, Orlie

Dear Folks, Love Orlie

▼

Camp Blanding, Florida

November 21, 1944

Dear Folks,

Just a few lines to let you know I'm okay and thinking of you. I sent you a telegram last night asking you for $75. I need it to help a friend out. He is shipping out and needs money to get his wife home. I know I'll get my money back soon so don't worry about it. He is an overseas returnee from the 34th. I have known him since I've been in the Army.

I wouldn't worry too much about my getting shipped back – at least not for awhile. I'm not worrying myself. I won't lie to them to keep from going even though I'd hate to go. Personally, I don't think I'll ever have to go back unless it's an emergency. Stimson couldn't possibly say they would keep us here because an emergency condition might arise and it would be a necessity to send us back.

I got a nice letter from Jo Popenhagen today. Also one from you and one from LaVonne. I've got an awful lot of letters to write if I ever get the time. Seems like I'm always so busy that I hardly have time to do anything.

The weather here is pretty cool just now. I have winter underwear on and it surely feels good. Well, folks, I guess I'd better close for this time. Write when you can.

Love,
Orlie

Orlie Meskimen

▼

Camp Gordon, Georgia

February 16, 1945

Dear Folks,

    As you have probably noticed by my return address I've been sent to another camp. I like it better here from what I've seen. The weather is nicer and the living quarters are a hundred percent better. I got my orders one day and moved the next. I'll tell you more about it in my next letter. I don't have much time right now.

    I don't know just how much this will affect my furlough but I'm afraid it will delay it some. They are organizing new outfits here so it may be some time before I'll be able to get one.

    I won't be getting paid until April so I'll have to have you send me $100 by return mail. I've got a number of things I'll have to buy and I'll need money until I get paid. Please send it as soon as possible.

    I hated to leave the other outfit but there was nothing I could do about it. I'll soon have new friends here anyway. Three of the fellows from my battalion at Blanding came along so I'll always be somewhere near them too.

    Well, folks, I guess I'd better close for this time. Write to me as soon as you can. Tell everyone hello for me.

Love,
Orlie

Dear Folks, Love Orlie

This is the last of Orlie's letters. It is believed that he finished the remainder of his service at Camp Gordon before being honorably discharged in July 1945.

EPILOGUE

Orlie was honorably discharged on July 6, 1945, with the rank of 1st Sergeant. Following his discharge he worked as a foreman at the Iowa Canning Company in Shellsburg and at Eddy Paper Company in Cedar Rapids until re-enlisting in the military in April 1947.

Orlie married LaVonne Marie Butler in October 1947. In November of that year he was stationed on the island of Guam where he served as Chief of the Security Branch in the Corps of Engineers. Orlie returned to the states in March of 1949. He re-enlisted and he and LaVonne relocated to California in November 1949, residing at the San Francisco Presidio. Orlie served as a Sergeant 1st Class in the 701st Military Police Battalion. He was promoted to the grade of Sergeant Major in October 1951. He and LaVonne's first child, Doug, was born there.

Orlie was awarded the following medals during the course of his military career:

Orlie Meskimen

- 3 Bronze Stars for exemplary service in ground combat against the armed enemy while assigned as first sergeant in the Mediterranean Theater of Operations
- Combat Infantry Badge
- European-African-Middle Eastern Campaign Medal
- Good Conduct Medal
- American Defense Medal
- French Croix de Guerre Medal with Palm

Orlie officially separated from military service in February 1953 in order to return to Iowa to care for LaVonne's terminally ill mother. Taking residence in Maquoketa, Iowa, Orlie worked as an account executive at Clinton Engines (Clinton Engines manufactured engines for washing machines, chain saws, outboard motors, industrial air circulation fans, and lawn mowers for a variety of companies; it manufactured machine gun components during World War II). He and LaVonne had four more children.

Clinton Engines filed for bankruptcy in 1966, and the family relocated to Beloit, Wisconsin, where Orlie was employed in sales at Fairbanks Morse Engines (Fairbanks Morse Engines manufactures a wide array of products including radios, washing machines, power mowers, water heaters, water softeners, air conditioners, and storage batteries).

In 1968 the family relocated to Genoa, Illinois, where

Dear Folks, Love Orlie

Orlie was employed in sales for Falls Products (Falls Products manufactured lawn mowers).

During his military career, Orlie was documented as experiencing exhaustion, shortness of breath, sinking spells when sleeping on his left side, and heart palpitations. These early health concerns, coupled with the combat conditions he endured in Africa and Italy, surely took a toll on his health. Orlie passed away at the age of 54 on June 4, 1973, from a massive heart attack.

These are his descendents:

1. Douglas James Meskimen (1950-2011)
2. Mary Lynn Meskimen-King (1953)
3. Steven Mark Meskimen (1954)
4. David Brian Meskimen (1956)
5. Ellen Rebecca Meskimen-Hustad (1959)